chatelaine
food express

# Quickies
## chicken

# Introduction

For all kinds of reasons, chicken is the perfect choice for our times. Its high-protein, low-fat content makes it a natural choice for these fat-conscious times, and its pleasing understated taste can quickly come alive with simple seasoning dress-ups and sassy sauces. You can do as much or as little as you like. *Quickies Chicken* provides endless combinations of glistening bastes, fresh sprinkles and devilishly hot sauces to add a little pizzazz to the naturally delicious flavor of chicken.

In about 15 minutes, for example, you can completely finish a flavorful entrée, providing you start with skinless, boneless chicken breasts. Or if you begin with chicken legs or thighs, the smarter budget choice, they too can be dressed up with homey sauces or hot 'n' spicy bastes, and made oven-ready in fewer than 15 minutes. Once the chicken is roasting in the oven, your work is over. Except for the eating and enjoying, of course.

So, no matter what you choose — boneless breasts, chicken pieces, wings or the whole bird — you can turn to page 8 for a recipe guide by chicken parts. For tips on safe cooking, boning and skinning of breasts and for nutritional information, see pages 138-39.

# Contents

# Recipe guide by chicken parts

At a glance, this handy guide presents all our recipes organized by chicken parts. They are divided according to cooking methods from Bakes and Barbecue to Sautés and Stir-Fries. In most cases preparation time is 15 minutes or less – sometimes only 5 minutes!

## Breasts, bone-in

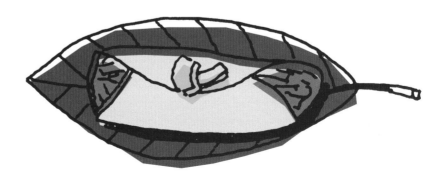

Quickies
chicken

# Breasts, skinless and boneless

recipe guide

## Chicken Livers

### Pasta
Sherried Chicken Livers, 66

### Stir-Fries
Peppery Liver Stir-Fry, 131

## Chicken Pieces

### Bakes
Baked Curried Coconut Chicken, 24
Crispy Crunchy Kid-Lovin' Chicken, 23
Oven-Fried Chili Chicken, 23

### One-Dish
Sassy Spanish-Style Chicken, 54
Soothing Chicken Fricassee, 54
Mexican Rice Supper, 55

### Roasts
Fire-Alarm Chicken, 77
Honey-Lime Chicken, 75

### Sautés
Spanish Chicken with Olives, 106
Tequila Margarita Chicken, 106

### Soups and Stews
Country French Leek & Chicken Soup, 113
Moroccan Chicken-Vegetable Soup, 111

## Cooked Chicken

### One-Dish
Rib-Sticking Express Pot Pie, 57

### Pasta
Asian Angel-Hair Slaw, 60
Linguine with Roasted Red Pepper & Smoked Chicken, 64

### Salads
Chicken Salad with Gorgonzola, 84
Curried Chicken Salad, 84
Great Chicken Caesar, 82
South Seas Chicken Salad, 84

### Sautés
Fast Curried Chicken, 105

### Soups and Stews
Easy Elegant Soup, 112

### Stir-Fries
Simply a Stir-Fry, 129

### Wraps
Baked Chicken Wraps, 134
Chicken Enchiladas, 134
Roasted-Chicken Fajitas, 135
Smoked Chicken Rolls, 135
Tropical Chicken Sandwich with Mango Mayonnaise, 137

## Ground Chicken

### Bakes
Creamy Mushroom Noodle Bake, 24
30-Minute Homemade Pizza, 25

### Burgers
Dijon Dill Burgers, 36
Moist Burgers with Cucumber Sauce, 36
Oriental Chicken Patties, 38
Parmesan Italian Burgers, 37
Savory California Burgers, 36
Tarragon Chicken Burgers, 38
Zucchini Jalapeño Burgers, 38

### Pasta
Curried Chicken 'n' Rice, 56
Fast Low-Fat Chicken Toss, 65
Fast Old-Fashioned Spaghetti, 66
Fast Spicy Mexican Lasagna, 56
Fettuccine à la King, 65

### Soups and Stews
Skillet Chicken Chili, 115

### Stir-Fries
Teriyaki Ground Chicken Stir-Fry, 127

### Wraps
Salsa-Spiked Rolls, 136

# Legs

## Bakes
Caesar-Parmesan Legs, 22
Crispy Taco Chip Chicken, 20
Fearless "Fried" Chicken, 21
Fiery Plum-Glazed Chicken, 14
Garlic-Ginger Chicken, 29
Ginger-Lime Legs, 22
Great Drumstick Bastes, 25
Italian Coated Legs, 22
Lusty Barbecued Wine Bake, 16
Oriental Legs, 20
Roasted Balsamic-Garlic Chicken, 20
Roast Salsa Chicken, 49

## One-Dish
Big-Batch Baked Chicken in Chili Sauce, 50
Moroccan Chicken & Rice, 53
Spicy "Southern Fried" Chicken & Chips, 52

## Roasts
Asian-Glazed Chicken, 74
Honey-Lime Chicken, 75
Roast Chicken & Spicy Oven Fries, 74

## Soups and Stews
Chicken Soup with Ginger, 111
Chicken with Wine & Olives, 118
Country Italian Chickpea Soup, 110
Garlic & Broccoli Chicken Soup, 114
Italian Chicken with Mushrooms, 118
Lemon Chicken Tagine, 122

# Thighs

## Bakes
Fiery Plum-Glazed Chicken, 14
Hoisin Ginger Thighs, 20

## Barbecue
Garlic-Ginger Chicken, 29
Herbed Citrus Thighs, 30

## One-Dish
Spicy "Southern Fried" Chicken & Chips, 52

## Roasts
Asian-Glazed Chicken, 74
Honey-Lime Chicken, 75
Roast Chicken & Spicy Oven Fries, 74

## Sautés
Classy Italian Sauté, 106
Curried Coconut Chicken, 102
Fast French Chicken Sauté, 104
Mexican Chicken Sauté, 104
Moroccan Tomato Sauté, 102
Presto Parmigiana Chicken Sauté, 103

# Whole Chicken

## Barbecue
Portuguese Chicken, 31

## Roasts
Caribbean Mango-Rum Chicken, 72
Classic Roast with Veggies, 70
Express Roast Chicken, 70
Lemon-Rosemary Chicken, 71
Roast Chicken with Caesar-Bacon Stuffing, 73
Roast Chicken with Fresh Thyme, 72
Spring Roast with Rice, 71

## Soups and Stews
Lemon Chicken Tagine, 122
Mediterranean Chicken, 122
Vin Blanc Coq au Vin, 120

# Wings

## Finger Foods
Caesar Wings, 42
Caribbean Citrus Wings, 42
Crunchy Tuscan Chicken Wings, 43
Finger-Lickin' Chicken, 43
Sizzling Wing Dips, 45
Suicide Wings, 42

# bakes

Chicken is incredibly easy to get along with. Just pop it into an oven dish and spoon a little olive oil, fresh lemon juice, garlic and dress-up herbs over top as we've done with these **Herbed Lemony Baked Breasts** (see recipe page 14). Then relax as it bakes to golden perfection and fills the kitchen with heady aromas.

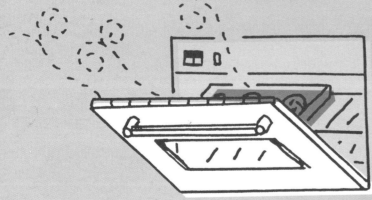

# chatelaine
## food express

# Quickies
## chicken

## Delicious ideas
## from bakes to wraps

## by Monda Rosenberg

**M&S**

A SMITH SHERMAN BOOK
produced in conjunction with CHATELAINE®
and published by McCLELLAND & STEWART INC.

# chatelaine

Canadian Cataloguing in Publication Data

Rosenberg, Monda
    Quickies Chicken: delicious ideas from bakes to wraps

(Chatelaine food express)
"A Smith Sherman book produced in conjunction with Chatelaine"
Includes index

ISBN 0-7710-7595-2

1. Cookery (Chicken). 2. Quick and easy cookery. I. Title. II. Series.
TX750.5.C45R67 2000          641.6'65        C00-930514-9

## acknowledgements

Few in life are lucky enough to find a team of workmates with whom they feel privileged to be associated. I've been blessed in this regard both in my collaboration with Smith Sherman Books Inc. in producing the Food Express series of cookbooks and in my association with my colleagues at CHATELAINE magazine. I owe great appreciation to Carol Sherman and Andrew Smith, who massage and manipulate our recipes into such appealing and beautiful books. Thanks to Joseph Gisini and Jonathan Freeman, who fine-tune every tiny detail of the design, Bernice Eisenstein for her flawless copyediting and Erik Tanner for all his help.

My sincere thanks also to the CHATELAINE Test Kitchen team, spearheaded by Trudy Patterson, who tested every recipe until they simply could not be improved upon; Deborah Aldcorn for her hawk-eyed editing; editor Rona Maynard for her constant caring and input; publisher Donna Clark, and director of marketing Mirabel Palmer-Elliot for their strong commitment to this project; the CHATELAINE creative team of art director Caren Watkins, senior associate art director Dave Donald and creative associate Barb Glaser; and our world-class photographer Ed O'Neil. Thanks to the entire McClelland & Stewart family, particularly editor Pat Kennedy for her constant support; and Alison Fryer and Jennifer Grange from the Cookbook Store for their sage advice.

MONDA ROSENBERG

COVER PHOTO: *TERRIFIC TERIYAKI SAUTÉ, see recipe page 97*
PHOTO PAGE 2: *BAKED CHICKEN WRAPS, see recipe page 134*
CREDITS: *see page 143*

bakes

## Herbed Lemony Baked Breasts

Lemon, basil and thyme give a burst of
fresh taste to this easy-bake chicken.

**PREPARATION: 5 MINUTES**
**BAKING: 45 MINUTES**

Preheat oven to 375°F (190°C). Whisk together
  2 tbsp olive oil
  2 tbsp freshly squeezed lemon juice
  1 minced large garlic clove
  1 tsp dried basil
  ½ tsp dried leaf thyme
  ¼ tsp salt
In a baking dish just large enough to hold them,
  place bone-side down
  4 skinless, bone-in chicken breasts
Pour sauce over chicken and bake, uncovered,
  basting often, until chicken feels springy,
  from 45 to 55 minutes.
*Makes: 4 servings*

## Zesty Greek Chicken

Roast and bake chicken in all the best tastes
of a terrific Greek salad dressing.

**PREPARATION: 10 MINUTES**
**BAKING: 40 MINUTES**

Preheat oven to 425°F (220°C). Whisk together
  grated peel of half a lemon
  ¼ cup freshly squeezed lemon juice
  1 tbsp olive oil
  3 minced large garlic cloves
  2 tsp dried leaf oregano
  ¼ tsp each salt and black pepper
Pour into a 9x13-inch (3-L) baking dish.
  Arrange bone-side up in mixture
  4 to 6 skinless, bone-in chicken breasts
Lay a piece of foil loosely over top. Bake for 20
  minutes. Turn chicken and baste. Reduce heat
  to 400°F (200°C). Continue baking,
  uncovered, basting every 10 minutes, from 20
  to 30 minutes. Serve chicken with pan juices.
*Makes: 4 to 6 servings*

## Fiery Plum-Glazed Chicken

This is the ultimate easy entrée.
And you probably have all the ingredients on hand
to make the sizzling sauce.

**PREPARATION: 10 MINUTES**
**BAKING: 45 MINUTES**

Preheat oven to 375°F (190°C). Place on a baking
  rack on a foil-lined pan
  6 skinless, bone-in breasts
    or legs or 8 thighs
Stir together
  1 cup plum sauce
  2 tbsp freshly squeezed lemon juice
  1 to 3 tsp hot pepper sauce
  2 minced large garlic cloves
    or 2 tsp bottled minced garlic
  1 tsp grated fresh or bottled minced ginger
  ¼ tsp salt
Spoon some, but not all, of the sauce over
  chicken. Spread to cover most of chicken,
  remembering as heat increases, sauce will
  run down sides. Bake for 30 minutes. Spoon
  on more sauce. Continue baking, spooning
  again with remaining sauce near end of
  baking, until chicken is done as you like,
  from 15 to 30 more minutes.
*Makes: 4 to 6 servings*

## Lime-Cumin Baked Breasts

Serve these succulent breasts with
saffron rice or couscous and lots of green onions.

**PREPARATION: 5 MINUTES**
**BAKING: 45 MINUTES**

Preheat oven to 375°F (190°C). Whisk together
    2 tbsp olive oil
    2 tbsp freshly squeezed lime juice
    1 minced large garlic clove
    1 tsp cumin
    ½ tsp paprika
    ¼ tsp salt
In a baking dish just large enough to hold them,
    place bone-side down
    4 skinless, bone-in chicken breasts
Pour sauce over chicken and bake, uncovered,
    basting often, until chicken feels springy,
    from 45 to 55 minutes.
    *Makes: 4 servings*

## Southwest Chicken

Chicken breasts are baked in a hot salsa
and white wine sauce for this relaxed dish.
Great with basil-scented potato wedges.

**PREPARATION: 10 MINUTES**
**BAKING: 45 MINUTES**

Preheat oven to 375°F (190°C). Stir together
    1 cup hot salsa
    ½ cup white wine
    3 tbsp vegetable oil
In a 9x13-inch (3-L) pan, arrange
    8 skinless, bone-in chicken breasts
Do not overlap them. Bake, uncovered, basting
    often, until chicken feels springy, about
    45 minutes.
    *Makes: 8 servings*

bakes

*Southwest Chicken*

bakes

## Lusty Barbecued Wine Bake

Mix red wine with your favorite barbecue sauce, then generously baste plump legs for this easy dinner.

**PREPARATION: 10 MINUTES**
**BAKING: 50 MINUTES**

Preheat oven to 350°F (180°C). In a bowl, stir together
  ½ cup bottled barbecue sauce, preferably smoky
  ½ cup dry red or white wine
In a large shallow baking dish, arrange
  5 skinless, bone-in chicken breasts or legs with thighs attached
Pieces must not be touching. Pour sauce over chicken and bake, uncovered and basting often, until golden, from 50 to 60 minutes. Pour sauce into a measuring cup. Spoon off and discard fat on top. Drizzle sauce over chicken or use for dipping. Perfect with baked potatoes.
*Makes: 5 servings*

## Spiced Caribbean Chicken

Just a rub of spices gives island heat to chicken. Remove skin from chicken for a low-fat number or leave on if you wish.

**PREPARATION: 5 MINUTES**
**BAKING: 45 MINUTES**

Preheat oven to 375°F (190°C). In a small bowl, stir together
  ½ tsp each cumin, curry, cinnamon and allspice
  ¼ tsp each nutmeg, salt and black pepper
Sprinkle over both sides of
  4 bone-in chicken breasts
Place in a shallow baking pan. Bake, uncovered, until well browned and chicken feels springy, about 45 minutes. Baste near end of baking. Serve with rice jazzed up with jalapeños, red peppers and sliced green onions.
*Makes: 4 servings*

## Teriyaki Chicken

Ginger and dry mustard give a peppery edge to this easy Asian coating.

**PREPARATION: 10 MINUTES**
**BAKING: 50 MINUTES**

Preheat oven to 350°F (180°C). Blend together
  1 tbsp melted butter
  1½ tsp dry mustard
In a shallow baking dish, place skin-side up
  4 bone-in chicken breasts (skin removed if you wish)
Generously brush with butter mixture. Bake, uncovered, for 20 minutes. Drain fat from pan. Stir together
  2 tbsp each soy sauce and liquid honey
  ¼ tsp each ground ginger and garlic powder
Pour over chicken. Bake, uncovered, 30 more minutes. Baste often.
*Makes: 4 servings*

# Easy Italian Bake

An incredibly easy dinner-in-a-dish that delivers down-to-earth taste for a mere 316 calories.

**PREPARATION: 10 MINUTES**

**BAKING: 1 HOUR**

Preheat oven to 400°F (200°C). Rub

1 minced garlic clove
   or a pinch of garlic powder

into

6 skinless, bone-in chicken breasts

Place in an oven dish just large enough to hold them. Scatter around chicken

2 onions, sliced into ½-inch (1-cm) wedges

Stir together

28-oz can diced or plum tomatoes,
   including juice

5½-oz can tomato paste

1½ tsp dried basil

½ tsp dried leaf oregano

pinches of salt and pepper

Pour over chicken and onions. Bake, uncovered, basting often, 40 minutes. Then sprinkle with

2 cups grated cheese,
   such as mozzarella or Asiago

Continue baking until cheese is golden, about 20 minutes. Remove chicken. Toss sauce with a cooked chunky pasta, such as shell or corkscrew, or spoon over rice and top with chicken.

*Makes: 6 servings*

**bakes**

*Easy Italian Bake*

bakes

## Parmesan Bruschetta Bake

Basil-scented tomatoes crown crispy Parmesan-coated chicken breasts – and no frying is needed. It's all done in a single baking dish.

**PREPARATION: 15 MINUTES**
**BAKING: 35 MINUTES**

Preheat oven to 375°F (190°C). In two separate bowls, have ready
  **¼ cup all-purpose flour**
  **2 beaten eggs**
Dip in flour, then in egg
  **4 skinless, boneless chicken breasts**
Arrange in a greased 9x13-inch (3-L) baking dish. Stir together
  **¼ cup finely grated Parmesan**
  **¼ cup store-bought fine dry bread crumbs**
Sprinkle evenly over chicken breasts. Loosely cover dish with foil and bake for 20 minutes. Meanwhile, slice in half
  **2 large ripe tomatoes**
  Squeeze out all juice and seeds. Chop pulp and toss together with
  **1 tbsp olive oil**
  **2 minced garlic cloves**
  **¼ cup chopped fresh basil or 1 tsp dried basil**
  **½ tsp salt**
  **¼ tsp freshly ground black pepper**
Uncover chicken and continue baking until crumbs are browned, from 12 to 15 more minutes. Heap tomato mixture on each breast and return to oven to just heat through, about 3 minutes. Excellent with potato wedges, lightly oiled and roasted along with the chicken.
*Makes: 4 servings*

## Low-Fat Curried Honey Breasts

Honey and Dijon make an amazingly rich coating for baked chicken.

**PREPARATION: 10 MINUTES**
**BAKING: 25 MINUTES**

Preheat oven to 350°F (180°C). Stir together
  **2 tbsp each liquid honey, ketchup and Dijon**
  **1 tsp curry powder**
  **¼ tsp cumin**
  **generous pinches of cayenne and salt**
  **3 thinly sliced green onions**
In a shallow baking dish, arrange
  **4 skinless, boneless chicken breasts**
Pour sauce evenly over chicken. Bake, uncovered, for 15 minutes. Turn and bake, basting often until chicken feels springy, 10 to 15 more minutes.
*Makes: 4 servings*

## Nana's Stuffing-Topped Creamy Chicken

From Tamara Mol of Grimsby, Ontario, comes her grandmother's recipe for a fast-fix "homey" dinner.

**PREPARATION: 15 MINUTES**
**BAKING: 1 HOUR**

Preheat oven to 350°F (180°C). Arrange in an ungreased 9x13-inch (3-L) baking dish
  **6 to 8 skinless, boneless chicken breasts**
Prepare according to directions on package
  **4-oz (120-g) box stuffing mix**
Spoon over chicken. Whisk together
  **10-oz can condensed cream of chicken soup**
  **½ cup milk**
Spoon over stuffing and spread slightly. In a single layer, lay over top
  **8-oz (250-g) pkg Swiss cheese slices, about 8 slices**
Bake until cheese is golden, about 1 hour.
*Makes: 6 to 8 servings*

# Summer Lemon Chicken

Perfect for baking a day ahead for a picnic
or patio dinner that's ready when you get home.

**PREPARATION: 15 MINUTES**
**BAKING: 1¼ HOURS**

Preheat oven to 325°F (160°C). Stir together
  **1 cup white wine**
  **coarsely grated peel and juice of 1 lemon**
  **3 minced garlic cloves**
    **or 1 tbsp bottled minced garlic**
  **1 tbsp chopped fresh rosemary**
    **or ½ tsp dried rosemary**
  **½ tsp salt**
Pour into an oven dish. Add and turn to coat
  **6 large skinless, boneless chicken breasts**
Scatter over chicken
  **1 thickly sliced large red onion,
    separated into rings**
Cover and bake for 30 minutes. Turn chicken.
  Cover again and continue baking another
  40 minutes. Sprinkle with
  **chopped fresh chives**
*Makes: 6 servings*

# Chicken Parmigiana

Here's all the much-loved Parmigiana flavor –
herbed chicken, spicy tomato sauce and melted
cheese – with a fraction of the usual fat and calories.

**PREPARATION: 10 MINUTES**
**BAKING: 25 MINUTES**

Preheat oven to 400°F (200°C). Remove any
  clinging fat from
  **4 skinless, boneless chicken breasts**
Lay between sheets of waxed paper. With the
  fleshy part of your fist, gently pound to flatten
  slightly. Rub all over with
  **2 tbsp low-fat Italian dressing**
Place coated breasts, overlapping if necessary, in
  a square 8-inch (2-L) dish or pan. Evenly top
  with, in the order given
  **½ cup thick spaghetti sauce**
  **pinches of dried basil and oregano
    or Italian seasonings**
  **¼ cup grated Parmesan**
  **½ cup grated mozzarella**
Cover dish with foil and bake for 15 minutes.
  Uncover and continue baking until cheese is
  golden, about another 10 minutes.
  Traditionally served over pasta.
*Makes: 4 servings*

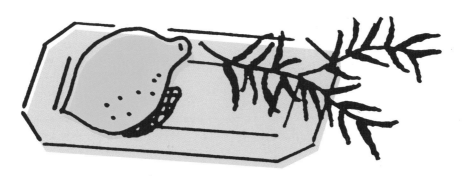

*Summer Lemon Chicken*

bakes

## Hoisin Ginger Thighs

Hoisin sauce adds an instant intriguing
depth of taste in this recipe.

**PREPARATION: 5 MINUTES**
**BAKING: 45 MINUTES**

Preheat oven to 350°F (180°C). In a bowl,
stir together
**¼ cup hoisin sauce**
**2 tbsp water**
**1 tbsp soy sauce**
**1 tsp freshly grated ginger**
**1 minced garlic clove**
In a baking dish, arrange in a single layer
**8 skinless chicken thighs**
Pour or brush sauce over chicken and bake,
uncovered, basting often, until chicken feels
springy, about 45 minutes.
*Makes: 4 servings*

## Oriental Legs

Sherry gives a sophisticated sweetness
to this effortless bake.

**PREPARATION: 5 MINUTES**
**BAKING: 1 HOUR**

Preheat oven to 350°F (180°C). In a small bowl,
stir together
**¼ cup each dry sherry and soy sauce**
**½ tsp ground ginger**
**3 minced garlic cloves**
**or 1 tsp bottled minced garlic**
In a shallow baking dish, arrange
**4 skinless chicken legs, thighs attached**
Pour sauce over chicken. Cover and bake for
30 minutes. Turn chicken and continue
baking, uncovered, basting often, until
chicken feels springy, about 30 more minutes.
*Makes: 4 servings*

## Roasted Balsamic-Garlic Chicken

A little balsamic vinegar is all it takes to add
a sweet 'n' sour zing to chicken.

**PREPARATION: 10 MINUTES**
**BAKING: 1 HOUR**

Preheat oven to 350°F (180°C). In a shallow
baking dish just large enough to hold them,
arrange fleshy side down
**4 chicken legs, thighs attached,**
**or skinless, bone-in chicken breasts**
Pour evenly over chicken
**3 tbsp balsamic vinegar**
Scatter around chicken
**6 peeled whole garlic cloves**
Cover and bake for 30 minutes. Turn chicken.
Continue baking, uncovered, basting
often, 30 more minutes. Remove chicken.
Mash garlic into vinegar mixture and
pour over chicken.
*Makes: 4 servings*

## Crispy Taco Chip Chicken

With a golden tortilla-chip coating, this recipe
beats take-out with the kids.

**PREPARATION: 10 MINUTES**
**BAKING: 1 HOUR**

Preheat oven to 375°F (190°C). In a plastic bag,
coarsely crush with a rolling pin or a heavy
can from the pantry
**½ (4-oz/120-g) pkg corn chips**
**or tortilla chips**
In a bowl, whisk together
**1 egg**
**2 tbsp water**
Roll in egg mixture, one at a time
**4 skinless chicken legs**
Then roll in crushed chips. Lay on a rack placed
on a baking sheet lined with foil or in a
broiling pan. Bake until golden, about 1 hour.
Serve with salsa and baked potatoes.
*Makes: 4 servings*

# Fearless "Fried" Chicken

Moist with a soft mellow Cajun taste, this oven-baked chicken will make you realize the high-fat fried variety pales in comparison. And all for 243 calories a serving.

**PREPARATION: 10 MINUTES**
**BAKING: 40 MINUTES**

Preheat oven to 425°F (220°C). Whisk together, then pour into a pie plate
- **1 egg white**
- **½ cup buttermilk**

Measure into a paper or plastic bag
- **½ cup all-purpose flour**
- **1 tsp each baking powder, paprika, dried leaf thyme, leaf oregano and salt**
- **½ to 1 tsp cayenne**

Close top and gently shake to mix. Remove any clinging fat from
- **4 skinless chicken legs or small bone-in chicken breasts**

Dip one piece into buttermilk mixture, then place in paper bag. Close top and shake gently to evenly coat. Place on a rack on a baking sheet with shallow sides. Repeat with remaining chicken. Discard flour mixture that did not cling to chicken. Using a pastry brush, evenly brush or dab over flour-coated chicken
- **2 tbsp vegetable oil**

This amount of oil is essential for a crispy crust. Bake, uncovered, until crisp and golden, from 40 to 45 minutes. Terrific with oven-fried chips and a crunchy coleslaw.
*Makes: 4 servings*

bakes

*Fearless "Fried" Chicken*

**bakes**

## Ginger-Lime Legs

A single juicy lime turns inexpensive
chicken legs into succulent fare.

**PREPARATION: 10 MINUTES**
**MARINATING: 1 HOUR**
**BAKING: 45 MINUTES**

Place in a baking dish just large enough to
hold them
**4 chicken legs (skin removed if you wish)**
Whisk together
**finely grated peel and juice of 1 lime**
**2 tbsp finely chopped or 1 tbsp grated**
**fresh ginger or ½ tsp ground ginger**
**1 tbsp vegetable oil**
**1 tbsp soy sauce**
**½ tsp hot pepper sauce**
**¼ tsp salt**
Pour over chicken. Cover and refrigerate for at
least 1 hour. Turn chicken at least once during
marinating. Preheat oven to 375°F (190°C).
Remove cover from dish and arrange
chicken, bone-side down. Bake, basting
often with pan juices, until chicken is golden
and feels springy, from 45 to 55 minutes.
*Makes: 4 servings*

## Italian Coated Legs

A crunchy treat with grown-up taste gets
a classy edge from freshly grated Parmesan.

**PREPARATION: 15 MINUTES**
**BAKING: 1 HOUR**

Preheat oven to 375°F (190°C). Line a broiling
pan or baking sheet with foil, then fit with
a rack. Stir together
**1 cup store-bought bread crumbs**
**or 2 cups fine fresh bread crumbs**
**¼ cup freshly grated Parmesan**
**1 tsp Italian seasoning or ½ tsp each**
**dried basil and leaf oregano**
**½ tsp salt**
Beat together
**1 egg**
**2 tbsp water**
Dip into egg mixture, then roll in bread-crumb
mixture
**6 chicken legs (skin removed if you wish)**
Lay on rack and bake until golden, about 1 hour.
*Makes: 6 servings*

## Caesar-Parmesan Legs

Only three ingredients are required here to
produce a substantial flavorful family supper.

**PREPARATION: 10 MINUTES**
**BAKING: 50 MINUTES**

Preheat oven to 350°F (180°C). Place in separate
bowls
**½ cup creamy Caesar dressing**
**½ cup freshly grated Parmesan**
One by one, thickly coat with dressing,
then Parmesan
**6 chicken legs, thighs attached**
To ensure crispness on all sides, place on a wire
rack set on a baking sheet. Cover loosely with
a tent of foil and bake for 30 minutes. Remove
foil and continue baking until golden and
cooked through, from 20 to 30 more minutes.
*Makes: 6 servings*

# Oven-Fried Chili Chicken

Moist chicken under a crunchy cornmeal
coating is ready in less than an hour.

**PREPARATION: 15 MINUTES**
**BAKING: 40 MINUTES**

Preheat oven to 325°F (160°C). Stir together
- ⅓ **cup each cornmeal and all-purpose flour**
- **2 to 3 tbsp sesame seeds (optional)**
- **3 tsp chili powder**
- ½ **tsp salt**
- **finely grated peel of 1 lemon**

Into a separate bowl, pour
- ⅔ **cup buttermilk**

Individually dip into buttermilk until coated
- **6 skinless, bone-in chicken pieces**

Then dip into cornmeal mixture. Press lightly
and turn to coat completely. Place on a lightly
oiled baking sheet. Bake chicken, uncovered,
until golden, from 40 to 45 minutes.
*Makes: 4 to 6 servings*

# Crispy Crunchy Kid-Lovin' Chicken

Kids love this protein-packed crispy chicken
and it's so easy, they can cook it themselves.

**PREPARATION: 5 MINUTES**
**BAKING: 1 HOUR**

Preheat oven to 375°F (190°C). Place in
two separate bowls
- ½ **(8-oz/250-mL) bottle flavorful salad**
  **dressing, such as creamy Caesar or Italian**
- **1 cup crushed cornflakes**

One at a time, coat in dressing
- **4 to 6 skinless, bone-in chicken pieces**

Then roll in crumbs and place on a baking sheet
lined with foil. Bake until golden and crisp,
about 1 hour. For an easy supper, bake
potatoes in the oven at the same time and
serve with steamed carrots and green beans.
*Makes: 4 to 6 servings*

**bakes**

*Crispy Crunchy Kid-Lovin' Chicken*

bakes

## Baked Curried Coconut Chicken

Here's delicious proof that a richly flavored curry can be simply stirred together, then tucked into the oven – no pot-sitting needed.

**PREPARATION: 20 MINUTES**

BAKING: 1¼ HOURS

Preheat oven to 375°F (190°C). Cut in halves or thirds
**8 large skinless, bone-in chicken pieces**
Arrange in a 9x13-inch (3-L) baking pan. Scatter over chicken
**1 finely chopped onion**
**1 finely chopped green pepper**
In a large bowl, stir together
**14-oz (400-mL) can coconut milk**
**1 cup chicken broth or bouillon**
**2 to 3 tbsp curry powder**
**2 tbsp freshly grated ginger**
**1 tbsp ground cumin**
**2 tsp ground coriander**
**¼ to ½ tsp hot red pepper flakes**
Pour over chicken and vegetables. Cover pan loosely with foil. Bake for 1¼ to 1½ hours, basting often with curry mixture and turning occasionally until chicken feels springy. Remove chicken. Spoon fat from top of sauce. Great with rice. It also freezes well.
*Makes: 8 servings*

## Creamy Mushroom Noodle Bake

Here's how to get old-fashioned chicken à la king without making a gooey cream sauce and roasting a big bird.

**PREPARATION: 10 MINUTES**

COOKING: 15 MINUTES

BAKING: 35 MINUTES

Preheat oven to 350°F (180°C). In a large frying pan over medium heat, melt
**2 tbsp butter**
Stir in
**1 lb (500 g) ground chicken**
**½ lb (250 g) sliced mushrooms**
Stir often, until chicken loses its pink color, about 10 minutes. Add
**2 cups chicken broth or bouillon**
**2 sliced celery stalks**
**¾ tsp ground nutmeg**
**½ tsp poultry seasoning or crumbled leaf sage**
**½ tsp salt**
Stir in
**1½ cups uncooked macaroni**
Bring to a boil. Then turn into a 2-quart (2-L) casserole dish. Cover tightly and bake in preheated oven for 25 minutes. Stir in
**2 cups frozen green peas**
Continue baking, covered, until peas are hot, about 10 minutes. Stir in
**1 cup light sour cream**
*Makes: 4 servings*

30-Minute Homemade Pizza

# 30-Minute Homemade Pizza

Freshly made pizza is definitely a cut above order in. Keep store-bought dough in the freezer so it's always handy.

**PREPARATION: 9 MINUTES**
**COOKING: 6 MINUTES  BAKING: 15 MINUTES**

Preheat oven to 425°F (220°C). Pat
   **1 lb (500 g) pizza or bread dough**
into a greased 9x12-inch (23x28-cm) baking
   sheet, forming a rim around edge.
In a frying pan over medium-high, heat
   **1 tbsp olive oil**
Add
   **½ lb (250 g) ground chicken**
   **1 chopped small onion**
   **1 minced large garlic clove**
Sauté, breaking up chicken as it cooks, until it
   loses all pink color, about 6 minutes. Stir in

**1 cup pizza or spaghetti sauce**
**1½ tsp Italian seasoning**
   **or 1 tsp basil and ½ tsp leaf oregano**
**¼ tsp black pepper**
**pinch of cayenne (optional)**
Spread evenly over crust and sprinkle with
   **2 cups grated mozzarella**
      **or mild provolone cheese**
   **¼ cup freshly grated Parmesan**
Bake immediately on bottom rack of oven until
   golden, from 15 to 20 minutes.
   *Makes: 14-inch pizza (8 wedges)*

# Great Drumstick Bastes

Chicken drumsticks are always a good buy, and oven-roasting is the easiest way to cook them.

Simply place 4 large legs in a shallow roasting pan and bake, uncovered, in a preheated 375°F (190°C) oven for 30 minutes. Then baste generously with one of the following delicious sauces. Continue baking for 15 to 20 more minutes, basting often with sauce.

### Great Garlic

Simmer **3 minced garlic cloves** in
   **2 tbsp each butter and olive oil**
   for about 5 minutes.

### Lemon-Pepper

Stir **2 tbsp melted butter** with
   **2 tbsp freshly squeezed lemon juice,**
   **½ tsp freshly ground black pepper** and
   **a pinch of salt.**

### Mexican Chili

Whisk **¼ cup ketchup** with
   **2 tbsp vegetable oil,**
   **1 minced garlic clove** and
   **1 tsp each chili powder and ground cumin.**

### Easy Caesar

Brush drumsticks with
   **⅓ cup vinaigrette-style Caesar salad dressing.**

### Hot BBQ

Stir **½ tsp hot pepper sauce** into
   **¼ cup of your favorite barbecue sauce.**

### Dilled Mustard

Whisk **1 tbsp Dijon** with
   **2 tbsp olive oil** and
   **½ tsp dried dillweed.**

### Zesty Curry

Whisk **¼ cup ketchup** with
   **¼ cup vegetable oil** and
   **2 tsp curry powder.**

# barbecue

It takes very little to add pizzazz to barbecued chicken.
Just grilling itself infuses a unique smoky essence. For
**Barbecued Fajitas** (see recipe page 28), we've basted
both the chicken and vegetables in a garlic-chili oil while
grilling, then crowned them with a jalapeño cream.
Besides the Southwestern attitude of these fajitas,
we also present fast ways to add Italian, Caribbean,
Portuguese, even Oriental overtones to your next grill.

**barbecue**

## Barbecued Fajitas

Grill the fixings for this restaurant-style fajita right on your own barbecue and lavishly drizzle with jalapeño cream. Serve bowls of colorful toppings so everyone can personalize their fajita.

**PREPARATION: 15 MINUTES**
**GRILLING: 15 MINUTES**

Oil grill and preheat barbecue to medium-high. Stir together
  **2 tbsp vegetable oil**
  **½ tsp chili powder**
  **¼ tsp each garlic salt and cayenne**
Lightly brush oil mixture over
  **4 skinless, boneless chicken breasts
    or 8 thighs**
  **3 sweet peppers, halved,
    preferably different colors**
  **1 thickly sliced red or Spanish onion**
Place on grill. Turning chicken once and vegetables often, grill, with lid closed, until chicken feels springy and vegetables are lightly charred, from 12 to 18 minutes. Meanwhile, stir together
  **½ cup light sour cream**
  **1 to 2 finely chopped seeded jalapeños**
As vegetables and chicken are done, remove to a cutting board and slice into strips. Warm on grill for 30 seconds per side
  **6 large flour tortillas**
Fill with chicken, vegetables and a dollop of sour cream mixture. Then roll up.
*Makes: 4 to 6 servings*

## Garlicky Butter Chicken

Start the grilling season with flair with this speedy rub-a-dub chicken.

**PREPARATION: 5 MINUTES**
**GRILLING: 14 MINUTES**

Oil grill and preheat barbecue. Mix together
  **finely grated peel of 1 lemon**
  **1 tsp curry powder**
  **½ tsp ground cumin**
  **¼ tsp salt**
Rub all over
  **4 skinless, boneless chicken breasts**
Lighty brush one side of chicken with
  **garlic butter or Garlicky Spread
    (see recipe page 89)**
Place coated-side down on barbecue. Grill for 8 minutes. Brush top with Garlicky Spread and turn. Brush again. Grill from 6 to 8 more minutes.
*Makes: 4 servings*

## Easy Kebab Appetizers

Use chutney in your marinade for a fast-fix way to this intriguing appetizer that is flavorful, yet not laden with fat or calories.

**PREPARATION: 10 MINUTES**
**GRILLING: 8 MINUTES**

Oil grill and preheat barbecue.
In a food processor, purée
  **½ cup apricot-and-ginger or mango chutney**
  **2 tbsp soy sauce**
  **1 tbsp each brown sugar and olive oil**
Turn into a bowl and stir in
  **6 skinless, boneless chicken breasts,
    cut into 1-inch (2.5-cm) pieces**
Thread skewers with chicken, alternating with pieces of
  **6 peppers, preferably a mix of colors, cut into
    1-inch (2.5-cm) pieces**
Place kebabs on grill. Barbecue, turning often, until chicken feels firm, from 8 to 10 minutes.
*Makes: 24 kebabs*

# Garlic-Ginger Chicken

Foil-packet cooking assures that you'll always end up with moist tender chicken.

**PREPARATION: 5 MINUTES**
**GRILLING: 50 MINUTES**

Oil grill and preheat barbecue. Stir together
1/4 cup room-temperature butter
1/4 cup liquid honey
3 minced garlic cloves
1 tsp ground ginger
Place individually on pieces of foil large enough
   to securely wrap
4 skinless, bone-in chicken breasts
   or drumsticks
Brush with garlic mixture. Seal foil and place packets on grill. Grill chicken, turning often, for 45 minutes. Remove packets from grill. Carefully open packets and pour hot juices into a bowl. Then remove chicken from foil and place directly on the greased grill. Barbecue, turning often, until chicken is golden brown, about 5 minutes. Baste frequently with reserved juices and watch carefully to avoid burning. Serve with remaining juice drizzled over chicken.
*Makes: 4 servings*

# BBQ Chicken & Lime

A 15-minute dip in marinade is all these breasts need for a succulent finish.

**PREPARATION: 10 MINUTES**
**MARINATING: 15 MINUTES**
**GRILLING: 10 MINUTES**

Place in a dish just large enough to hold them
   or in a large self-sealing bag
4 skinless, boneless chicken breasts
Stir together
   finely grated peel and juice of 1 lime
   2 tbsp olive or vegetable oil
   1 tbsp liquid honey
   2 minced large garlic cloves
   1/2 tsp ground thyme
   generous pinches of salt and black pepper
Pour over chicken and leave at room temperature for about 15 minutes or refrigerate for several hours.
Oil grill and preheat barbecue. Remove chicken from marinade and place on grill. Barbecue until chicken feels springy, from 5 to 8 minutes per side.
*Makes: 4 servings*

*Easy Kebab Appetizers*

**barbecue**

# Cumin Chicken Salad

Cumin adds flavor without overpowering in this main-course salad. Avocado adds creaminess.

**PREPARATION: 15 MINUTES**
**GRILLING: 12 MINUTES**

Stir together
  1 tbsp vegetable oil
  1 tbsp ground cumin
Rub or brush all over
  3 skinless, boneless chicken breasts
Place in a dish, cover and refrigerate. In a bowl, whisk together
  ⅓ cup vegetable oil
  2 tbsp freshly squeezed lemon juice
  1½ tbsp Dijon
  1½ tsp ground cumin
  ½ tsp salt
  ¼ tsp black pepper
Stir in
  2 chopped seeded tomatoes
  1 finely chopped small shallot
Set dressing aside. In a large bowl, combine
  1 to 2 heads romaine lettuce, torn into
    bite-size pieces (about 16 cups)
  3 thinly sliced green onions
Oil grill and preheat barbecue. Grill chicken until springy, from 6 to 8 minutes per side. Thinly slice chicken into strips. Add warm chicken to salad mixture. Whisk dressing and toss with salad. Sprinkle with
  1 cubed avocado
*Makes: 4 servings*

# Herbed Citrus Thighs

Tender boneless chicken thighs are a great buy and always filled with lots of flavor.

**PREPARATION: 20 MINUTES**
**MARINATING: 2 HOURS**
**GRILLING: 16 MINUTES**

Stir together
  1 cup orange juice
  ½ cup freshly squeezed lemon juice
  2 tbsp olive oil
  ½ cup chopped fresh basil
    or 1 tbsp dried basil
  ¼ cup chopped fresh oregano
    or 1 tsp dried leaf oregano
  2 minced garlic cloves
  ¾ tsp salt
  ½ tsp freshly ground black pepper
In a glass dish or self-sealing plastic bag, place
  8 skinless, boneless thighs
Add marinade and cover dish or seal bag.
  Marinate in refrigerator for at least 2 hours or overnight. Turn once during marinating. Then oil grill and preheat barbecue. Grill thighs until golden, from 8 to 10 minutes per side. Brush often with marinade, except for last 5 minutes of grilling. Marinade can be boiled for 5 minutes and used as a dipping sauce. Serve with a rice pilaf and a Greek salad.
*Makes: 4 servings*

# Portuguese Barbecued Chicken

This chicken may need a little more time, but it's tangy, spicy and a deep golden brown.

**PREPARATION: 15 MINUTES**

**COOKING: 5 MINUTES   MARINATING: 3 HOURS   GRILLING: 1 HOUR**

In a small saucepan over medium, heat

   ¼ cup olive oil

Stir in

   1½ to 3 tsp hot red pepper flakes

Remove from heat and stir in

   1 cup white wine

   ¼ cup freshly squeezed lemon juice

   4 minced garlic cloves

   2 tbsp paprika

   2 tbsp white vinegar

   1 tsp freshly ground black pepper

   ¾ tsp salt

Remove skin from

   2 chickens, about 3½ lbs (1.75 kg) each

Slash chicken in several spots to a depth of about ¼ inch (0.5 cm) so oil mixture can penetrate meat. Place chickens in two large self-sealing plastic bags. Add oil mixture, making sure it covers chickens. Seal bags. Refrigerate for at least 3 hours, preferably overnight. Turn bags at least once.

Oil grill and preheat barbecue. Drain chickens, saving marinade. Place bone-side down on barbecue. Grill with lid closed, brushing often with marinade for 30 minutes, turn and continue barbecuing without basting until chicken is springy, about 30 minutes more.

*Makes: 6 to 8 servings*

*Portuguese Barbecued Chicken*

barbecue

**chatelaine**
food express

barbecue

# Fresh Herb Marinade

This marinade is perfect for any cut of chicken, even wings. Just marinate chicken in the refrigerator for an hour or two before cooking.

**PREPARATION: 15 MINUTES**

In a bowl, whisk together
- ⅓ cup olive oil
- 2 tbsp hazelnut oil (optional)
- 2 tbsp freshly squeezed lemon juice
- 1 minced garlic clove
- generous pinches of salt and black pepper

Stir in
- ¼ cup finely chopped parsley sprigs
- ¼ cup shredded basil leaves

Remove leaves from
- 5 sprigs of thyme

Coarsely chop leaves and add to marinade. Cover. Leave marinade at room temperature for at least 30 minutes to blend flavors.

*Makes: ⅔ cup*

# Grilled Tomato Relish

For an assertive warm relish, perfect for chicken, just grill a few tomatoes along with your chicken and toss with balsamic vinegar and green onions.

**PREPARATION: 15 MINUTES**
**GRILLING: 7 MINUTES**

Lightly oil grill and preheat barbecue.
Lightly brush oil all over
- 10 ripe but firm plum tomatoes, about 2 lbs (1 kg), sliced in half lengthwise

Barbecue for 4 to 5 minutes, then turn. Continue barbecuing until tomatoes are hot, but not soft, 3 to 5 more minutes. For a smokier flavor, close barbecue lid while grilling. Move tomatoes to a cutting board, then chop into ¼-inch (0.5-cm) pieces.

Stir together
- 3 thinly sliced green onions
- 2 tbsp olive oil
- 1 tbsp balsamic vinegar
- ½ tsp freshly ground black pepper
- ¼ tsp salt

Add grilled tomatoes. Stir until well mixed.

*Makes: 3 cups*

Grilled Tomato Relish

# tips
## barbecue without burning

Chicken is a challenge to barbecue because of its delicate meat and irregular thickness. By the time the centre of a piece of chicken still on the bone is thoroughly cooked, the outside is often burned. To avoid this, precook chicken pieces in the microwave or oven, or in foil on the barbecue. Then for irresistible barbecue flavor, place chicken directly on the barbecue for 10 to 15 minutes, turning often, until chicken is golden on the outside. Always keep the barbecue lid down or cover with a tent of aluminum foil. Brush with sauce if you want.

**Oven Method:** Place chicken pieces in a covered dish or wrap 1 or 2 pieces individually in foil and bake in preheated 375°F (190°C) oven for 45 minutes. Then barbecue for 10 to 15 minutes.

**Barbecue Method:** Wrap pieces individually in foil and place on the grill for about 45 minutes, turning often. Then remove foil and place directly on grill for 10 to 15 minutes.

**Microwave Method:** Arrange chicken pieces in a microwave-safe dish, in a single layer, with thickest parts toward the outside. Cover loosely with waxed paper or plastic wrap. Microwave on high for 6 to 8 minutes per pound, turning and rearranging pieces halfway through. Cover and refrigerate until ready to grill, or immediately place on the barbecue over medium heat. Coat with barbecue sauce and turn chicken frequently. Most pieces will need about 10 minutes set directly on the barbecue grill over medium heat.

# burgers

Chicken burgers are a smart light, yet high protein, alternative to beef – a 3-oz (90-g) patty comes with a mere 173 calories but a whopping 18 grams of protein. And there's no big trick to preparing and serving them up – just keep them away from high heat. *Moist Chicken Burgers with Cucumber Sauce* (see recipe page 36) are a great introduction. Studded with garlic, a handful of green onions and coriander and a special sour cream cucumber sauce, they're great any night of the week.

burgers

## Moist Chicken Burgers with Cucumber Sauce

These burgers are not only flavor-packed but low-fat as well. A healthy whopper with lots of creamy sauce rings in at only 273 calories.

**PREPARATION: 20 MINUTES**
**COOKING: 12 MINUTES**

Mix together
- **1 lb (500 g) ground chicken**
- **1 beaten egg**
- **¾ cup soft bread crumbs, about 2 slices bread**
- **2 tbsp finely chopped fresh coriander**
- **2 thinly sliced green onions**
- **1 minced garlic clove**
- **½ tsp salt**
- **¼ tsp cayenne**

Shape into 4 patties, each about ½ inch (1 cm) thick. In a large nonstick frying pan over medium, heat
- **1½ tsp vegetable oil**

Add burgers. Brown on both sides, about 4 minutes per side. Then reduce heat to medium-low, cover and cook from 2 to 4 more minutes per side. Serve burgers topped with a dollop of Cucumber Sauce (see recipe page 39) along with green beans. Or serve on whole-grain rolls topped with lettuce and tomato.
*Makes: 4 burgers*

## Savory Californian Burgers

Add West Coast glamour to your burgers with ingredients you probably already have in the pantry.

**PREPARATION: 10 MINUTES**
**COOKING: 12 MINUTES**

Blend together with a fork or your hands
- **1 lb (500 g) ground chicken**
- **finely grated peel of half an orange**
- **1 tbsp Dijon**
- **½ tsp each dried sage leaves and salt**
- **¼ tsp cayenne or black pepper**

Shape into 4 patties, each about ½ inch (1 cm) thick. In a large nonstick frying pan over medium-low, heat
- **2 tsp vegetable oil**

Add burgers and sauté, uncovered, until juices run clear, from 6 to 10 minutes per side. Or place burgers on a greased grill and barbecue with lid down until juices run clear, from 6 to 8 minutes per side.
*Makes: 4 burgers*

## Dijon Dill Burgers

Ground chicken struts its stuff in these fast light burgers.

**PREPARATION: 10 MINUTES**
**COOKING: 12 MINUTES**

Stir together until blended
- **1 egg**
- **½ tsp each Dijon and dried dillweed**
- **¼ tsp each salt and white pepper**

Add
- **2 lbs (1 kg) ground chicken or turkey**

Blend together with a fork or your hands. Form into 8 patties, each about ½ inch (1 cm) thick. In a large nonstick frying pan, heat
- **2 tsp butter**

Add half the patties. Cook over medium-low heat, covered, from 6 to 10 minutes per side. Repeat with remaining patties.
*Makes: 8 burgers*

# Parmesan Italian Burgers

These chicken burgers are incredibly moist and not high in fat.

**PREPARATION: 10 MINUTES**

**COOKING: 12 MINUTES**

Whisk together until blended
- **1 egg**
- **¼ cup freshly grated Parmesan**
- **½ tsp Italian seasoning**
- **generous pinch of garlic powder
  or 1 minced garlic clove**
- **¼ tsp salt**

Add and work with a fork until blended
- **1 lb (500 g) ground chicken**

Shape into 4 patties, each about ½ inch (1 cm) thick. In a wide nonstick frying pan, heat
- **2 tsp olive oil or butter**

Add burgers and cook over medium heat, uncovered, until light golden, about 4 minutes per side. Reduce heat to medium-low, cover and cook from 2 to 4 more minutes per side. Place burgers in warm pitas or crusty buns and spoon Incredibly Fast Salsa (see recipe page 88) over top.
*Makes: 4 burgers*

burgers

*Parmesan Italian Burgers*

## Tarragon Chicken Burgers

Creamy Dijon and assertive tarragon give seductive French flavor to these burgers.

**PREPARATION: 10 MINUTES**
**COOKING: 12 MINUTES**

In a bowl, whisk together
- **1 egg**
- **¼ cup light sour cream**
- **1½ tsp Dijon**
- **1 tsp dried tarragon**
- **½ tsp salt**
- **¼ tsp white pepper**

Add and work with a fork until blended
- **1 lb (500 g) ground chicken**
- **3 thinly sliced green onions**
- **¼ cup store-bought fine dry bread crumbs**

Shape into 4 patties, each about ½ inch (1 cm) thick. In a large frying pan over medium-low, melt
- **1 tbsp butter**
- **1 tsp vegetable oil**

Add burgers and sauté, covered, until browned and no pink remains in centre, from 6 to 10 minutes per side. Serve on a toasted bun with a coating of sour cream, a few sliced tomatoes and mesclun green leaves.
*Makes: 4 burgers*

## Zucchini Jalapeño Burgers

Zucchini is always a good buy at the supermarket. Here grated zucchini combines with lean ground chicken for moist burgers.

**PREPARATION: 10 MINUTES**
**GRILLING: 14 MINUTES**

Whisk together
- **1 egg**
- **finely grated peel of half a lemon**
- **½ tsp salt**
- **generous pinch of white pepper or cayenne**

Stir in
- **1 lb (500 g) ground chicken or turkey**
- **1 grated small zucchini, squeezed dry**
- **¼ cup store-bought fine dry bread crumbs**
- **1 finely chopped seeded jalapeño**
- **1 sliced green onion**

Form into 4 patties, each about ¾ inch (2 cm) thick. Barbecue on a greased grill, covered, until well done, from 7 to 12 minutes per side. Tuck in rolls with sliced tomatoes.
*Makes: 4 burgers*

## Oriental Chicken Patties

A little white wine gives an elegant edge to these inexpensive patties.

**PREPARATION: 10 MINUTES**
**COOKING: 17 MINUTES**

Crumble into a bowl and mix briefly
- **1½ lbs (750 g) ground chicken or turkey**
- **¼ tsp each salt and pepper**

Form into 4 to 6 patties, each about ¾ inch (2 cm) thick.

In a frying pan over medium-low, heat
- **2 tsp sesame oil**

When hot, add patties and cook, covered, from 6 to 10 minutes per side. Patties should be light golden and firm. Transfer to a plate, cover and keep warm. Add to pan
- **½ cup white wine**
- **2 tsp fresh grated ginger**
  **or a pinch of ground ginger**
- **1 tsp soy sauce**
- **¼ tsp sugar**

Bring to a boil over medium-high heat. Stir often, uncovered, until reduced to about ⅓ cup, about 5 minutes. Spoon over patties and sprinkle with
- **3 thinly sliced green onions**
*Makes: 4 to 6 burgers*

## Sassy Toppings

Add extra zing to your burgers with these flavourful garnishes.

### Curried Dijon

Mix **2 tbsp Dijon** and **2 tbsp sour cream** with **¼ tsp cumin or curry powder**. Wonderful over chicken, beef and lamb burgers.

### Cucumber Sauce

Grate and squeeze the juice from **¼ English cucumber**. Blend with **1 cup light sour cream or thick yogurt, 2 tbsp chopped fresh coriander** and **1 tsp grated lemon peel**. Spoon over chicken, fish or burgers.

### Perfect Pickle Relish

Finely chop **1 large dill pickle**. Stir with **2 tbsp mayonnaise, 1 tbsp chopped green onion** and **¼ tsp hot pepper sauce**. Drizzle over chicken, fish and beef burgers.

### Spanish Sauce

Stir **½ cup salsa** with **½ cup sliced stuffed green olives, ¼ cup finely chopped Spanish onion** and **1 crushed garlic clove**. Great over chicken, fish and beef burgers.

**burgers**

## tips

# ground control

**Burger Basics:** When making burgers or meatballs with poultry, add some light flavor perks, such as Dijon, fresh dill, a pinch of basil, poultry seasoning, tarragon, lemon pepper, ground cumin or coriander. Since ground chicken creates softer burgers and meatballs than beef, add an egg and dry bread crumbs to hold them together. Adding a little sauce, such as tomato or sour cream, will also keep patties moist. Because they're soft, they can be a challenge to flip on the barbecue. They're much easier to sauté.

**Lighten Up:** To liven up your favorite burger recipe, use ground chicken instead of beef. Since a 3-oz (90-g) serving of ground chicken has about 173 calories, compared with 248 for regular ground beef, you'll cut calories and slash the fat by a third. Just substitute one for the other in spaghetti sauce, lasagna, tacos, shepherd's pie, even tourtière.

### Burger Flavor Boosters

• finely chopped fresh herbs, such as chives and coriander, are healthy taste additions.

• add instant fiery flavor with cayenne, dried chilies, hot pepper sauce or salsa.

• grated cheese — especially crumbled feta, chèvre, Stilton, smoked cheese or aged cheddar — adds soothing flavor.

• finely grated onion or zucchini, or finely chopped shallots, hot peppers or green onions add taste and juiciness.

# finger foods

Begin your next video or backyard party with a platter of chicken nibblers. Whether curry 'n' coconut coated fingers, slim rosemary kebabs or the *Caribbean Citrus Wings* pictured here (see recipe page 42), chicken appetizers are always the first to go from the cocktail buffet. Just don't forget the cold beer and napkins.

chatelaine
food express

**finger foods**

## Caribbean Citrus Wings

Here's an easy "island" baste that makes these wings perfect nibbles for a patio party.

**PREPARATION: 5 MINUTES**
**MARINATING: 1 HOUR**
**BAKING: 30 MINUTES**

Preheat oven to 375°F (190°C). Cut and discard wing tips from

**2 lbs (1 kg) large chicken wings**

Slice wings in half at joint. Place in a single layer in a dish or in self-sealing plastic bag. In a bowl, stir together

**½ cup frozen orange juice concentrate**
**¼ cup soy sauce**
**1 tsp allspice**
**½ tsp cayenne**

Pour sauce over wings. Cover dish or seal bag, then refrigerate for at least 1 hour, preferably overnight. Turn halfway through marinating. Lift wings from marinade and place on a rack set on a foil-lined baking sheet. Bake, uncovered, for 20 minutes. Turn wings and baste with remaining marinade. Continue roasting until wings are richly glazed and golden brown, from 10 to 20 more minutes, depending on size of wings.
*Makes: 6 appetizer servings*

## Caesar Wings

These wings capture the addictive flavor of Caesar salad, including the essential blend of dressing ingredients and Parmesan.

**PREPARATION: 15 MINUTES**
**BAKING: 25 MINUTES**

Preheat oven to 375°F (190°C). Cut and discard wing tips from

**2 lbs (1 kg) large chicken wings**

Slice wings in half at joint. In a small bowl, stir together

**2 cups vinaigrette-style Caesar dressing**
**3 tbsp finely grated Parmesan**
**1 tsp freshly ground black pepper**

Brush chicken wings liberally with mixture. Arrange wings on a rack on a foil-lined baking sheet. Wings should not be touching. Bake, basting occasionally, for 15 minutes. Then turn wings and brush with any remaining mixture. Continue baking until chicken is tender, from 10 to 20 more minutes, depending on size of wings.
*Makes: 6 appetizer servings*

## Suicide Wings

A triple pepper treat earns these wings a "5 chili" designation.

**PREPARATION: 15 MINUTES**
**BAKING: 25 MINUTES**

Preheat oven to 375°F (190°C). Cut and discard wing tips from

**2½ lbs (1.25 kg) large chicken wings**

Slice wings in half at joint. In a large bowl, stir together

**⅔ cup spaghetti sauce**
**2 tbsp vegetable oil**
**4 finely chopped garlic cloves**
**1 tbsp liquid honey**
**1 tsp hot pepper sauce**
**½ tsp hot red pepper flakes**
**¼ tsp cayenne**

Add chicken pieces and stir until coated. Arrange wings on a rack on a foil-lined baking sheet. Wings should not be touching. Bake for 15 minutes. Turn wings and brush with remaining sauce. Continue baking until chicken is tender, from 10 to 20 minutes, depending on size of wings.
*Makes: 8 appetizer servings*

# Crunchy Tuscan Chicken Wings

Here's a crispy wing nibbler that's
not hot 'n' fiery but irresistible.

**PREPARATION: 15 MINUTES**
**BAKING: 30 MINUTES**

Preheat oven to 375°F (190°C). Stir together
- **1 cup store-bought bread crumbs
  or 2 cups fine fresh bread crumbs**
- **¼ cup freshly grated Parmesan**
- **1 tsp Italian seasoning
  or ½ tsp each dried basil and leaf oregano**
- **½ tsp salt**

Beat together
- **1 egg**
- **2 tbsp water**

Cut and discard wing tips from
- **2 lbs (1 kg) large chicken wings**

Slice wings in half at joint. Dip wings into egg
mixture, then roll in bread-crumb mixture.
Arrange wings on a rack on a foil-lined
baking sheet. Bake until golden, from
15 to 25 minutes per side, depending
on size of wings.

*Makes: 6 appetizer servings*

# Finger-Lickin' Chicken

Salsa and soy are an unlikely,
but dynamite, duo in this wing coating.

**PREPARATION: 10 MINUTES**
**BAKING: 25 MINUTES**

Preheat oven to 375°F (190°C). Cut and discard
wing tips from
- **2 lbs (1 kg) large chicken wings**

Slice wings in half at joint. Arrange wings on a
rack on a foil-lined baking sheet. The pieces
should not be touching. In a small bowl,
stir together
- **½ cup salsa or chili sauce**
- **2 tbsp soy sauce**
- **1 tbsp each brown sugar and vegetable oil**
- **2 tsp Worcestershire**

Brush chicken wings generously with half the
mixture. Bake for 15 minutes. Then turn
wings and brush with remaining sauce.
Continue to bake until chicken is cooked
and skin is crispy, from 10 to 20 more
minutes. Serve with sour cream for dipping.

*Makes: 6 appetizer servings*

finger foods

Crunchy Tuscan Chicken Wings

## Easy Curry 'n' Coconut Chicken Fingers

It would be hard to pack more Caribbean tastes into these elegant fingers.

**PREPARATION: 15 MINUTES**
**BAKING: 25 MINUTES**

Preheat oven to 400°F (200°C).
Slice into finger-size strips
**2 skinless, boneless chicken breasts**
Mix together
**½ cup light sour cream**
**¼ tsp curry powder**
Coat chicken pieces with sour cream mixture and roll in
**½ cup shredded unsweetened coconut**
Arrange coated pieces on a rack on a foil-lined baking sheet about ½ inch (1 cm) apart. Bake, uncovered, for 15 minutes. Turn each piece and continue baking until golden and crisp, about 10 to 15 more minutes.
*Makes: 10 fingers*

## Tangy Dijon Chicken Fingers

Skip the deep frying and bake 'em instead!

**PREPARATION: 15 MINUTES**
**BAKING: 25 MINUTES**

Preheat oven to 400°F (200°C).
Slice into finger-size strips
**2 skinless, boneless chicken breasts**
Mix together
**3 tbsp Dijon**
**3 tbsp light mayonnaise**
Coat chicken pieces with sauce, then roll in
**crushed cornflakes or bread crumbs**
Arrange coated pieces on a rack on a foil-lined baking sheet about ½ inch (1 cm) apart. Bake, uncovered, for 15 minutes. Turn each piece and continue baking until golden and crisp, from 10 to 15 more minutes.
*Makes: 10 fingers*

## Sautéed Chicken Fingers

Group these cayenne treats around a bowl of blue cheese dressing for dipping.

**PREPARATION: 10 MINUTES**
**COOKING: 7 MINUTES**

Slice into finger-size strips
**2 skinless, boneless chicken breasts**
Stir together
**2 tbsp flour**
**pinches of salt, cayenne and ground oregano**
Coat chicken pieces in seasonings.
In a large frying pan, melt
**1 tbsp butter**
Add several chicken pieces and sauté over medium heat, turning often, until golden, about 7 to 8 minutes. Repeat with remaining pieces. Serve drizzled with
**lemon juice**
*Makes: 10 fingers*

# Mini Rosemary-Lemon Kebabs

The olive oil and lemon marinade in this recipe is so good you'll probably want to use it on thighs and breasts.

**PREPARATION: 20 MINUTES**
**MARINATING: 1 HOUR   BAKING: 15 MINUTES**

In a medium-size glass bowl, whisk together
- ½ **cup olive oil**
- finely grated peel of **1 lemon**
- ¼ **cup freshly squeezed lemon juice**
- 1 tsp **dried crushed rosemary**
- ¼ tsp **salt**
- ¼ to ½ tsp **cayenne**

Slice into 1-inch (2.5-cm) cubes
- 8 **skinless, boneless chicken breasts**

Place in marinade. Stir until evenly coated. Cover and refrigerate for at least 1 hour or up to 4 hours. Preheat oven to 375°F (190°C). Loosely thread 2 marinated chicken cubes each onto small skewers. Place kebabs, at least 1 inch (2.5 cm) apart, on a rack set in a shallow baking pan. Discard any remaining marinade. Bake until chicken feels springy, about 15 minutes. Serve with mayonnaise spiked with cayenne.

*Makes: 34 mini kebabs*

finger foods

## tips
# winging it

### Wing Basics

- For fast, even cooking, separate wings at the joints. Remove the tips and freeze them — they make terrific chicken stock.

- For thorough marinating, place wings and marinade in a plastic bag. Seal and place bag in a bowl. Refrigerate and turn bag or massage it periodically so marinade coats all the pieces. For a fast marinade, use a bottled vinaigrette.

- When making your own brush-on bastes, add some vegetable oil to prevent burning and to keep food moist. Keep the sugar content low because it burns easily.

- For crisp skin, place chicken on a rack set in a baking pan, instead of directly on the pan. For easy clean-ups, line the baking pan with foil or parchment paper before baking.

### Sizzling Wing Dips

Add zing to your wings with these dips:

- Mash blue cheese into sour cream.

- Stir honey and fresh or ground ginger into sour cream or yogurt.

- Mix equal amounts of mayonnaise with yogurt or sour cream. Stir in your favorite spices, such as basil, oregano or thyme.

- Stir Dijon into mayonnaise.

- Add a hot pepper sauce, such as Tabasco or hot garlic-chili, or Worcestershire sauce into your favorite bottled barbecue sauce.

- Stir sour cream and salsa together.

- Use bottled creamy salad dressings, such as blue cheese, cucumber, Greek feta or Caesar.

# one-dish

Pull out your prettiest casserole dishes for our line-up of uncomplicated one-dish dinners. From aromatic pot pies like this **Cornmeal-Crusted Pot Pie** (see recipe page 48) to a robust Mexican lasagna, these uncomplicated entrées all produce homey-flavored meals sure to gratify the heartiest of appetites. Many can be made completely ahead, ready for your next gathering.

one-dish

## Cornmeal-Crusted Pot Pie

Bake chicken in a smoky pepper-spiked sauce under a golden cornmeal crust in two simple steps.

**PREPARATION: 30 MINUTES**
**BAKING: 55 MINUTES**

Preheat oven to 375°F (190°C). In a large bowl, mix with a spatula
  ¼ cup all-purpose flour
  ½ cup each smoky-flavored barbecue sauce and tomato sauce
Stir into flour mixture until coated
  6 skinless, boneless chicken breasts, quartered
Then stir in
  28-oz can drained diced tomatoes
  2 coarsely chopped green peppers
  2 finely chopped seeded jalapeños or 1 tsp hot red pepper flakes
  4 minced garlic cloves
  1½ tsp each cumin and ground coriander
  ½ tsp each dried leaf oregano and cinnamon
Turn into a 9x13-inch (3-L) baking pan. Press down to level and evenly distribute mixture. Drape dish with foil. Bake for 30 minutes.

CORNMEAL TOPPING
After 20 minutes baking, in a bowl, using a fork, stir together
  1½ cups cornmeal
  ¾ cup all-purpose flour
  2 tbsp granulated sugar
  4 tsp baking powder
  ½ tsp each salt and black pepper
Stir in
  ⅔ cup grated old cheddar
In another bowl, whisk together
  2 eggs
  ¼ cup vegetable oil
  1 cup milk

Stir into cornmeal mixture just until all ingredients are moistened.
After chicken mixture has baked 30 minutes, remove chicken from oven. Drop large dollops of cornmeal mixture over chicken. Smooth evenly to cover casserole. Return to oven. Bake, uncovered, until golden and sauce bubbles around edges, from 25 to 30 minutes. Let stand 5 minutes before serving.
*Makes: 6 to 8 servings*

## Spanish Chicken with Rice

Here's a fast-track route to a colorful complete dinner.

**PREPARATION: 15 MINUTES**
**COOKING: 30 MINUTES**

In a large wide saucepan over medium, heat
  1 tbsp olive oil
Add
  1 coarsely chopped large onion
  2 minced garlic cloves
Cook, stirring often, for 2 minutes. Stir in
  28-oz can whole plum tomatoes, including juice
  ¾ cup uncooked rice
  ½ cup sliced pimento-stuffed green olives
  ½ tsp dried leaf thyme
  ¼ tsp dried leaf oregano
Break up tomatoes. Cover and bring to a boil. Meanwhile, slice into bite-size pieces
  4 skinless, boneless chicken breasts
Stir into rice mixture. Cover tightly. Simmer over low heat, stirring often, until rice is cooked, about 25 minutes.
*Makes: 4 servings*

## Roast Salsa Chicken

A sassy saucy roast chicken dinner, complete with vegetables,
takes a lot less work than you think.

**PREPARATION: 10 MINUTES**
**ROASTING: 40 MINUTES**

Preheat oven to 400°F (200°). In a large greased baking pan with shallow sides, place, skin-side up
   **3 to 4 bone-in chicken breasts or legs**
Spread over chicken
   **1 cup thick salsa, hot or medium**
Scatter around chicken
   **2 to 3 unpeeled potatoes, cut into big French-fry wedges**
Cover pan with foil, sealing only two sides. Bake chicken for 15 minutes. Uncover and baste chicken. Stir potatoes to coat with juices. Continue baking, uncovered, 15 more minutes. Scatter over chicken
   **2 sweet peppers, sliced into strips, or 4 small zucchini, sliced into bite-size pieces**
Continue roasting from 10 to 15 more minutes. Sprinkle with
   **½ cup fresh coriander**
*Makes: 2 to 3 servings*

one-dish

*Roast Salsa Chicken*

**one-dish**

## Big-Batch Baked Chicken in Chili Sauce

This easy-bake chicken feeds a big casual gathering royally and is even wonderful reheated.

**PREPARATION: 20 MINUTES**
**BAKING: 1½ HOURS**

Preheat oven to 375°F (190°C). In a large roasting pan, arrange bone-side down
**12 skinless, bone-in chicken breasts or legs**
Sprinkle with
**2 tbsp chili powder**
**¼ tsp salt**
Scatter with
**2 coarsely chopped onions**
**2 coarsely chopped sweet peppers**
**2 (19-oz) cans drained red kidney beans**
Stir together
**28-oz can diced tomatoes, including juice**
**14-oz can tomato sauce**
**1 cup barbecue sauce, preferably smoky-flavored**
**2 finely chopped seeded jalapeños**
**3 minced garlic cloves**
**1 tbsp each ground cumin and ground coriander**
**1 tsp each dried leaf oregano and cinnamon**
Pour over chicken. Drape dish with foil. Do not seal. Bake for 1½ hours, stirring and turning chicken after 1 hour. Serve with a spinach salad of mesclun greens and spinach.

*Makes: 12 servings*

## Roasted Lemon-Garlic Chicken & Veggies

Roasting garlic tames its assertive flavor, making it buttery. Prepare a complete dinner here in one dish.

**PREPARATION: 20 MINUTES**
**BAKING: 55 MINUTES**

Preheat oven to 375°F (190°C). Whisk together
**½ cup white wine**
**2 tbsp olive oil**
**1 tbsp liquid honey**
**finely grated peel of 1 lemon**
**1 tbsp freshly squeezed lemon juice**
**½ tsp salt**
**¼ tsp cayenne**
Then stir in
**¼ cup finely chopped fresh basil or coriander or 2 tbsp chopped fresh rosemary, thyme or oregano**
Pour into a large 11x13-inch (28x33-cm) broiling pan. Add and turn to coat, then place bone-side up
**6 skinless, bone-in chicken breasts**
Place around chicken, turning to coat with wine mixture
**1 whole head of garlic, separated into cloves but not peeled**
**1 lb (500 g) julienned carrots or parsnips**
**1 head fennel, with stems trimmed, then thinly sliced**
**3 unpeeled potatoes, sliced in half**
Roast, uncovered, for 30 minutes. Turn breasts. Baste with pan juices. Stir vegetables. If more liquid is needed, add
**½ cup wine**
Continue baking, basting often, until chicken feels springy, from 25 to 30 more minutes. Remove chicken and vegetables. Squeeze garlic from peel, mash with a fork and stir into pan juices with
**½ cup light sour cream (optional)**
Drizzle over chicken.

*Makes: 6 servings*

# Oven BBQ Southern Chicken 'n' Spuds

Beer-laced barbecue sauce gives a sumptuous grill taste to this indoor roast dinner.

**PREPARATION: 15 MINUTES**

**BAKING: 45 MINUTES**

Preheat oven to 375°F (190°C). In a large broiler pan lined with foil, place
- 4 skinless, bone-in chicken breasts
- 4 large cooking onions, quartered

Then toss together to coat
- 4 sweet potatoes, peeled and cut into wedges
- 1 to 2 tbsp olive oil
- 1 tsp dried rosemary

Arrange around chicken. Stir together
- ½ cup bottled barbecue sauce
- ⅓ cup beer

Generously brush over chicken and onions, saving some sauce. Bake, uncovered, from 45 to 55 minutes, brushing chicken and onions often with remaining sauce.

*Makes: 4 servings*

**one-dish**

*Oven BBQ Southern Chicken 'n' Spuds*

## Spicy "Southern Fried" Chicken & Chips

There's no deep-fat frying needed for this healthy take on New Orleans-style crispy chicken and chips.

**PREPARATION: 15 MINUTES**
**BAKING: 45 MINUTES**

Place one oven rack at lowest level and one just above oven centre. Preheat oven to 425°F (220°C). Toss together
  - 4 unpeeled baking potatoes, sliced into wedges
  - 2 tbsp vegetable oil
  - generous pinches of salt and freshly ground black pepper

Spread out on an oiled baking sheet. In a pie plate, whisk together with a fork
  - 1 egg white
  - ¼ cup light sour cream
  - ¼ cup skim milk

Shake together in a closed plastic bag
  - ½ cup all-purpose flour
  - 1 tsp each baking powder, salt, ground cumin and chili powder
  - ½ to 1 tsp cayenne

Dip individually into milk mixture to coat
  - 4 skinless, bone-in chicken breasts or legs or 8 thighs

Then place in plastic bag, close top and shake to evenly coat. Shake off excess flour. Lay coated chicken on a baking rack placed on a broiling pan. Repeat with remaining chicken. Discard any flour mixture left in bag. Using a pastry brush, lightly brush or dab over flour coating on chicken
  - vegetable oil (1 tbsp total)

This is essential for a crispy crust. Bake chicken on lowest rack and potatoes on upper rack of oven until chicken is crisp and potatoes are fork-tender, about 45 minutes. Turn potatoes every 15 minutes.
*Makes: 4 servings*

## French Tarragon Casserole

Toasted rice and tarragon add flair to a wholesome chicken supper.

**PREPARATION: 15 MINUTES**
**COOKING: 30 MINUTES**
**BAKING: 1 HOUR**

Preheat oven to 350°F (180°C). In a large ungreased frying pan over medium heat, pour
  - 1 cup uncooked rice

Stir occasionally until golden, about 5 minutes. Pour into a 2-quart (2-L) casserole dish with
  - 2 chopped celery stalks

In a large frying pan over medium heat, melt
  - 1 tbsp butter

Add bone-side up
  - 4 bone-in chicken breasts (skin removed if you wish)

Sauté until golden, about 10 minutes. Remove chicken. Drain most of fat from pan. Add
  - 1 sliced large onion
  - 1 minced garlic clove
  - 3 chopped carrots
  - ½ lb (250 g) sliced mushrooms, about 4 cups

Sauté until onion softens, about 5 minutes. Add
  - 1 cup chicken broth or bouillon
  - ¾ tsp dried tarragon
  - pinches of salt and cayenne

Stir until any browned bits on bottom are taken into liquid and mixture boils. Stir into rice. Top with chicken, browned side up. Cover and bake until rice and chicken are cooked, about 1 hour.
*Makes: 4 servings*

# Moroccan Chicken & Rice

The North African love of a slight sweetness
in savory dishes works well in this streamlined chicken-and-rice casserole.

**PREPARATION: 15 MINUTES**

**COOKING: 10 MINUTES    BAKING: 1 HOUR**

Preheat oven to 375°F (190°C). In a large frying pan, heat
- **1 tbsp olive oil**

Add and stir often over medium heat, 5 minutes
- **1 chopped large onion**
- **3 thinly sliced carrots**
- **4 minced garlic cloves**

Stir in
- **2 cups chicken broth or bouillon**
- **¾ cup orange juice**
- **1 tsp each cinnamon, cumin and nutmeg**
- **¼ tsp salt**

Bring to a boil. Then stir in
- **1½ cups rice, preferably long grain**

Spread mixture in a 9x13 (3-L) baking dish. On top, place bone-side down
- **6 skinless, bone-in chicken breasts or legs**

Cover and bake, 30 minutes. Stir together
- **2 tbsp orange juice**
- **1 tbsp honey**
- **¼ tsp each cinnamon, cumin and nutmeg**

Uncover chicken. Brush with some of mixture. Bake for 15 minutes. Brush again. Continue baking until chicken feels springy, another 15 minutes. Remove chicken. Stir into rice
- **4 sliced green onions**

*Makes: 6 servings*

*Moroccan Chicken & Rice*

one-dish

one-dish

## Soothing Chicken Fricassee

Cherry tomatoes and minced cloves of sautéed garlic add fresh zing to this fricassee, a main event for Friday night, whether or not company is coming.

**PREPARATION: 25 MINUTES**
COOKING: 1 HOUR

In a large wide saucepan over medium, heat
  **2 tbsp vegetable oil**
  **1 tbsp butter**
Add and brown in several batches
  **4 lbs (2 kg) bone-in chicken pieces**
  **(skin removed if you wish)**
Set chicken aside. Remove all but 3 tablespoons fat from pan. Add
  **4 peeled shallots (if large, cut in half)**
  **1 chopped medium-size onion**
  **2 sliced carrots**
  **2 chopped celery stalks**
  **2 minced garlic cloves**
Sauté over medium heat, stirring often, until vegetables just start to turn brown, from 3 to 4 minutes. Pour in
  **½ cup dry white wine**
Gently scrape bottom of pan to remove any brown bits. Place chicken back in pan. Sprinkle with
  **1 tsp dried leaf thyme**
  **½ tsp poultry seasoning**
  **generous pinches of salt and black pepper**
Add
  **2 cups chicken broth or bouillon**
Cover and simmer, turning chicken several times, until cooked through, about 45 minutes. If serving right away, add during last minutes of cooking
  **½ pint cherry tomatoes (optional)**
Fricassee can be refrigerated for 1 day or frozen. If making ahead, add cherry tomatoes when reheating.
*Makes: 4 servings*

## Sassy Spanish-Style Chicken

Everyday pantry ingredients go international in this easy simmering dish.

**PREPARATION: 20 MINUTES**
COOKING: 50 MINUTES

Sprinkle
  **6 skinless, bone-in chicken pieces**
with
  **salt and pepper**
In a large saucepan over medium, heat
  **1 tbsp olive oil**
Add chicken but do not overcrowd pan. Cook until well browned on both sides, about 10 minutes. Remove to a plate. Discard all but 1 tablespoon fat from saucepan. Add
  **2 coarsely chopped celery stalks**
  **1 chopped onion**
  **1 chopped green pepper**
Stir often until lightly browned, about 7 minutes. Stir in
  **28-oz can drained diced tomatoes**
  **½ cup sliced stuffed green olives**
  **½ cup red wine**
  **½ tsp each dried leaf thyme and dried leaf oregano**
  **¼ tsp cayenne**
When boiling, add chicken to pan. Reduce heat to low and cover. Cook until chicken feels springy, turning once, from 30 to 40 minutes. Great over rice or noodles.
*Makes: 4 to 6 servings*

## Mexican Rice Supper

This is a good candidate for a potluck dinner. Teenagers particularly love it.

**PREPARATION: 20 MINUTES**

**COOKING: 10 MINUTES  BAKING: 1¼ HOURS**

Preheat oven to 350°F (180°C). In a small bowl, stir together

- **1½ tsp each cumin, chili powder and ground coriander**
- **¼ tsp each salt and black pepper**

Pour half of this mixture into another bowl. Rub remaining all over

- **6 skinless, bone-in chicken pieces**

In a large frying pan over medium, heat

- **1 tbsp vegetable or olive oil**

Add chicken. Cook, turning once, until golden, about 10 minutes. Meanwhile, in a 9x13-inch (3-L) pan, stir together

- **1 cup uncooked long-grain rice**
- **2 cups chicken broth or bouillon**
- **2 chopped zucchini**
- **1 chopped onion**
- **1 chopped red pepper**
- **½ cup corn kernels**

Stir in remaining seasonings. Top with browned chicken. Tightly cover dish and bake for 1 hour. Uncover and sprinkle with

- **2 cups grated Monterey Jack, Swiss or mozzarella cheese**

Continue baking, uncovered, until cheese is golden, from 10 to 15 more minutes.
*Makes: 6 servings*

one-dish

*Mexican Rice Supper*

one-dish

## Curried Chicken 'n' Rice

Ground chicken, curry and sour cream come together to form the perfect creamy topping for rice.

**PREPARATION: 15**
**COOKING: 9 MINUTES**

In a saucepan over medium-high, combine
- **1 lb (500 g) ground chicken**
- **2 finely chopped onions**
- **½ cup water**
- **1 chicken bouillon cube, crumbled**
- **2 tsp curry powder**

Cook, uncovered, stirring often, until most of liquid has evaporated, from 6 to 8 minutes. Stir in
- **2 cups frozen green peas**

Cover and cook until peas are hot, from 3 to 5 minutes. Stir in
- **1 cup yogurt or light sour cream**

Serve on cooked rice or broad noodles.
*Makes: 4 servings*

## Fast Spicy Mexican Lasagna

Tortillas replace lasagna noodles, and salsa makes an instant sauce in this easy-to-bake Southwestern-style lasagna.

**PREPARATION: 30 MINUTES**
**COOKING: 15 MINUTES**
**BAKING: 35 MINUTES**

In a saucepan over medium, sauté for 5 minutes
- **1 tbsp vegetable or olive oil**
- **2 chopped onions**

Add, bring to a boil, then remove from heat
- **1½ cups salsa**
- **14-oz can tomato sauce**
- **2 tsp ground cumin**

In a large oiled frying pan, combine
- **1 chopped onion**
- **2 minced garlic cloves**
- **1½ lbs (750 g) ground chicken**

Sprinkle with
- **2 tbsp chili powder**
- **½ tsp salt**

Stir often over medium heat for 10 minutes. Stir in
- **2 chopped green peppers**

Remove pan from heat. Preheat oven to 375°F (190°C). Lightly oil a 9x13-inch (3-L) baking dish. Spread a thin layer of tomato sauce over bottom. Cut in half and arrange over sauce
- **5 tortillas**

Spread with about 1 cup of sauce. Top with half of chicken mixture. Spread with
- **1 cup light or regular sour cream**

Slice in half and form another layer with
- **5 tortillas**

Spread with remaining chicken mixture, then tomato sauce. Sprinkle with
- **2 cups grated Monterey Jack or mozzarella cheese**

Bake until cheese is golden, from 35 to 40 minutes. Let stand 10 minutes before cutting.
*Makes: 8 to 10 servings*

# Rib-Sticking Express Pot Pie

With about 10 minutes of prep, you can create an amazing comforting deep-dish pie.

**PREPARATION: 10 MINUTES**
**BAKING: 35 MINUTES**

Preheat oven to 400°F (200°C). In a saucepan over medium, whisk together
> **10-oz (284-mL) can condensed cream of chicken or celery soup**
> **½ cup light sour cream**
> **1 tsp each poultry seasoning and Dijon**

Meanwhile, rinse with cold water until ice crystals are melted
> **1-lb (500-g) pkg frozen mixed or stir-fry vegetables, about 6 cups**

Drain well, then stir into soup mixture with
> **2 cups bite-size pieces cooked chicken**

Cook, stirring often, until hot, about 5 minutes. Turn into a deep 3-quart (3-L) casserole dish or 10-inch (25-cm) baking dish and level top.

Then stir together
> **2 cups biscuit mix**
> **½ cup grated cheddar**

Stir in just enough to moisten
> **⅓ to ½ cup milk**

Drop by spoonfuls over hot filling. The entire surface will not be covered. Sprinkle with
> **½ cup grated cheddar**

Bake, uncovered, until bubbling and biscuits are golden, about 25 minutes.
*Makes: 6 to 8 servings*

one-dish

*Rib-Sticking Express Pot Pie*

# pasta

This section presents clever ways to marry our two most popular dinner staples – chicken and pasta – including this exotic *Asian Angel-Hair Slaw* tossed with a sesame-lime dressing (see recipe page 60). As well as the traditional Italian pastas, some of the recipes use the popular Oriental noodles and no-cook rice noodles.

chatelaine
food express

pasta

## Asian Angel-Hair Slaw

Pasta salad takes on a whole new taste and look when you use Oriental ingredients such as fish sauce and sesame oil.

**PREPARATION: 20 MINUTES**
COOKING: 9 MINUTES

In a large pot of boiling salted water, cook until al dente, from 5 to 8 minutes
  **½ (1-lb/450-g) box angel-hair**
    **or spaghettini pasta**
Drain and rinse under cold water. Drain again. Meanwhile, in a large mixing bowl, combine
  **2 to 3 grated carrots**
  **2 finely sliced green onions**
  **3 cups finely shredded napa**
    **or green cabbage**
  **½ cup chopped fresh coriander or basil**
  **2 cups shredded cooked chicken**
In a small bowl, whisk together
  **2 tbsp vegetable oil**
  **1 tbsp dark sesame oil**
  **1 tbsp fish sauce**
  **finely grated peel of 1 lime**
  **1 tbsp freshly squeezed lime juice**
  **2 minced garlic cloves**
  **1 tsp granulated sugar**
  **½ tsp hot red pepper flakes**
Place well-drained pasta on top of vegetables and chicken. Whisk dressing again and pour over pasta. Toss until evenly mixed. Salad will keep well, covered and refrigerated, for 1 day.
*Makes: 5 to 8 servings*

## Stir-Fry Primavera

Your pantry and refrigerator probably contain all the ingredients you need for this superb number.

**PREPARATION: 10 MINUTES**
COOKING: 13 MINUTES

In a large pot of boiling salted water, cook until nearly al dente, from 7 to 8 minutes
  **½ lb (250 g) spaghetti**
    **or fresh Oriental noodles**
  (If using Oriental noodles, cook no more than 2 to 3 minutes.)
Meanwhile, in a small bowl, stir together
  **3 tbsp oyster sauce**
  **1½ tsp each soy sauce and dark sesame oil**
  **½ tsp hot red pepper sauce**
    **or hot garlic-chili sauce**
In a large wide frying pan or wok over medium-high, heat
  **1 tbsp peanut or vegetable oil**
When hot, add
  **4 skinless, boneless chicken breasts, sliced into thin strips**
Stir-fry for 2 minutes. Add
  **2 sliced green onions**
  **1 each julienned red pepper and yellow pepper**
Continue stir-frying until vegetables are nearly tender, about 2 more minutes. Stir in sauce mixture and stir-fry from 2 to 3 minutes, until chicken is cooked. Add drained pasta and toss until coated.
*Makes: 4 servings*

# Curried Shrimp & Oriental Noodles

The ultimate spring curry — light, colorful and teeming with many tastes and textures, yet just 491 calories per serving. It's great served hot or cold.

**PREPARATION: 15 MINUTES**
**COOKING: 15 MINUTES**

Place in a large bowl and cover with boiling water
　½ (1-lb/454-g) pkg broad rice noodles
Stir well, then soak, while continuing with recipe, from 10 to 15 minutes. In a large deep frying pan over medium, heat
　1 tbsp peanut or other vegetable oil
Add
　2 finely chopped seeded jalapeños
　2 minced garlic cloves
Stir constantly for 2 minutes. Add
　4 skinless, boneless chicken breasts, each sliced lengthwise into 5 strips
Sprinkle with
　1 tbsp ground cumin
　2 tsp curry powder
　½ tsp hot red pepper flakes
　¼ tsp salt

Stir frequently for 3 minutes. Add
　2 sweet peppers, preferably 1 red and 1 green, cut into 1-inch (2.5-cm) triangles
　½ cup chicken broth or bouillon
　½ lb (250 g) large uncooked shrimp, shelled and deveined
Stir often until chicken feels springy, from 5 to 6 minutes. Stir in
　3 thinly sliced green onions
　1 cup bean sprouts
　½ cup light sour cream
If using cooked shrimp, add now. Stir until warmed through. Add drained rice noodles and toss.
*Makes: 4 to 6 servings*

*Curried Shrimp & Oriental Noodles*

pasta

## Sesame Noodles

Add snow peas, asparagus pieces or broccoli to this chicken delight and dinner is done.

**PREPARATION: 10 MINUTES**
**COOKING: 10 MINUTES**

In a large pot of boiling salted water, cook until al dente, about 10 minutes
   ½ (1-lb/450-g) pkg spaghetti or linguine
Meanwhile, in a medium-size bowl, whisk together
   2 tbsp soy sauce
   1 tbsp cornstarch
   ½ tsp sesame oil
Stir in until coated
   3 skinless, boneless chicken breasts, cut into bite-size strips
In a large frying pan over medium, heat
   1 tbsp peanut or vegetable oil
   1 tsp freshly grated ginger
      or bottled minced ginger
   1 minced large garlic clove
      or ½ tsp bottled minced garlic
Stir constantly for 2 minutes. Add coated chicken and stir until chicken feels springy, from 4 to 5 minutes. Stir in
   3 thinly sliced green onions
Drain pasta and add to frying pan. Sprinkle with
   1 tbsp soy sauce
   ½ tsp sesame oil
Toss until evenly mixed.
   *Makes: 2 to 3 servings*

## Celebration Spring Pasta

In the spring, you want an excuse to buy all that glorious-looking asparagus and fresh basil. Let them star in this pretty pasta toss.

**PREPARATION: 10 MINUTES**
**COOKING: 15 MINUTES**

In a large pot of boiling salted water, cook until al dente, from 10 to 12 minutes
   1-lb (450-g) pkg bow tie, penne
      or rotini pasta
Meanwhile, in a large nonstick frying pan over medium-high, heat
   1 tbsp olive oil
Add
   2 skinless, boneless chicken breasts, cut into bite-size pieces
Stir-fry until cooked, 5 to 7 minutes. Remove chicken to a plate.
Add to pan
   10-oz can undiluted chicken broth
   ½ cup dry white wine
   1 tbsp dried basil (if using fresh, add later)
Stir together, then add to pan
   ¼ cup dry white wine
   2 tbsp cornstarch
Whisk constantly until thickened, about 3 minutes. Add
   ¾ lb (375 g) fresh asparagus, woody bottoms removed, cut into ½-inch (1-cm) pieces
   1 sliced yellow or green zucchini
   1 sliced yellow bell pepper
   2 cups frozen peas or fresh sugar snap peas
Reduce heat to medium and stir often until tender-crisp, about 5 minutes. Add chicken. When hot, toss with drained pasta and
   ½ cup shredded fresh basil
      (if using instead of dried)
   ½ cup grated Parmesan
   *Makes: 6 servings*

# Singapore Shrimp & Noodles

In just 20 minutes you can make this gorgeous stir-fry – as good as any from a fine Oriental restaurant.

**PREPARATION: 20 MINUTES**
COOKING: 15 MINUTES

Place in a large bowl and cover with boiling water
   ½ (1-lb/500-g) pkg rice-stick noodles
Stir well, then soak, while continuing with
   recipe, from 10 to 15 minutes. In a large
   nonstick frying pan over medium-high, heat
   1 tbsp vegetable oil
Add
   1 minced garlic clove
   1 julienned sweet pepper
   2 tsp curry powder
   pinch of hot red pepper flakes
   2 tbsp water
Stir for 2 minutes. Add
   2 skinless, boneless chicken breasts,
      sliced into bite-size pieces

Stir often for 5 minutes. Then add
   ½ lb (250 g) uncooked medium shrimp,
      shelled
Stir until pink, about 2 minutes. Add
   ½ cup chicken broth or bouillon
   ¾ tsp salt
When boiling, stir in softened well-drained
   noodles along with
   ¼ lb (125 g) snow peas, cut in half if large
   2 cups bean sprouts
   4 sliced green onions
   1 tbsp sesame oil, preferably dark
Stir often until hot.
   *Makes: 6 servings*

pasta

*Singapore Shrimp & Noodles*

**pasta**

## Presto Chicken Cacciatore

We've updated this much-loved classic.
It's still as yummy, but it takes just 30 minutes
from stove to table.

**PREPARATION: 12 MINUTES**
**COOKING: 18 MINUTES**

In a large pot of boiling salted water, cook until
al dente, from 8 to 12 minutes
**½ (1-lb/450-g) pkg broad egg noodles**
Meanwhile, in a large oiled frying pan over
medium-high, sauté until light golden, from
3 to 4 minutes per side
**2 large or 4 small skinless, boneless
chicken breasts**
Add
**½ chopped small onion**
Stir until just beginning to soften, about
2 minutes. Stir in
**½ small green pepper
or 1 celery stalk, chopped
1½ cups sliced mushrooms
2 cups spaghetti sauce
¼ cup white wine
2 bay leaves**
When bubbling, cover and adjust heat so
mixture gently bubbles. Cook until
chicken feels springy, about 10 minutes.
Turn chicken partway through and stir
sauce often. Remove bay leaves. Serve over
hot drained noodles.
*Makes: 2 to 4 servings*

## Linguine with Roasted Red Pepper & Smoked Chicken

A simple sauce gets smoky flavor from
freshly roasted peppers, which now come
conveniently in a jar.

**PREPARATION: 20 MINUTES**
**COOKING: 15 MINUTES**

In a large pot of boiling salted water, cook until
al dente, from 8 to 10 minutes
**¼ (1-lb/450-g) pkg linguine
or fettuccine**
Meanwhile, purée and set aside
**4 roasted red peppers or 10-oz (313-mL)
jar roasted red peppers, drained**
Then in a frying pan over medium-high, heat
**2 tbsp olive oil**
Add
**½ lb (250 g) sliced mushrooms
2 minced garlic cloves
¾ tsp salt
½ tsp sugar
pinch of cayenne**
Stir fry until mushrooms lose most of their
moisture, about 5 minutes. Stir in puréed
peppers with
**2 cups coarsely chopped cooked
or deli-smoked chicken**
When hot, toss with hot drained pasta and
**2 thinly sliced green onions**
Serve immediately with grated Parmesan.
*Makes: 1 to 2 servings*

## Fettuccine à la King

Here's a modern take on chicken à la king. The creaminess and comfort are still here, but it's low-fat now.

**PREPARATION: 10 MINUTES**
**COOKING: 12 MINUTES**

In a large pot of boiling salted water, cook until al dente, about 8 minutes
**½ (1-lb/450-g) pkg fettuccine**

Meanwhile, in a frying pan over medium, melt
**1 tbsp butter**

Crumble into pan
**1 lb (500 g) ground chicken**

Stir often, until chicken is cooked through, from 5 to 8 minutes.

Stir in and heat through
**1 cup light sour cream**
**4 thinly sliced green onions**
**½ tsp poultry seasoning**
**¼ tsp nutmeg**

Then toss with cooked drained pasta and
**½ cup Parmesan**
*Makes: 3 to 4 servings*

## Fast Low-Fat Chicken Toss

Ground chicken punches up prepared spaghetti sauce in record time.

**PREPARATION: 15**
**COOKING: 11 MINUTES**

In a wide deep saucepan over medium heat, combine
**1 lb (500 g) ground chicken**
**¼ cup water**

Cook, uncovered, stirring often, until most of liquid has evaporated, about 6 minutes. Add
**2 cups store-bought spaghetti sauce, preferably with mushrooms**
**2 finely chopped celery stalks (optional)**
**½ tsp Italian seasoning or dried tarragon (optional)**
**¼ tsp cayenne (optional)**

Cover, reduce heat to low and simmer, stirring often, 5 minutes. Toss with
**3 cups hot cooked fettuccine**
*Makes: 4 servings*

**pasta**

*Fettuccine à la King*

## Fast Old-Fashioned Spaghetti

Create old-fashioned taste with gusto yet using only 5 ingredients.

**PREPARATION: 15 MINUTES**
**COOKING: 12 MINUTES**

In a wide frying pan, place
  ½ lb (250 g) ground chicken
Into the pan, drain juice from
  19-oz can Italian-style stewed tomatoes
Cook over medium heat, working with a fork, until meat loses its pink color, about 4 minutes. Add stewed tomatoes and
  1 cup spaghetti sauce
  1 tsp hot red pepper flakes
Simmer, uncovered, stirring often, for 5 minutes. Add
  1 chopped green pepper
Continue simmering, uncovered, stirring often, until pepper is tender-crisp, 3 more minutes. Toss with hot cooked spaghetti.
*Makes: 4 cups sauce for 2 servings*

## Sherried Chicken Livers

If you adore chicken livers, here's the fast route to an extremely satisfying dinner.

**PREPARATION: 10 MINUTES**
**COOKING: 10 MINUTES**

In a large pot of boiling salted water, cook until al dente, from 8 to 10 minutes
  ½ (1-lb/450-g) pkg broad noodles
Meanwhile, in a frying pan, heat
  2 tbsp butter
When bubbling, add
  ½ lb (250 g) chicken livers, halved
Sauté over medium heat just until they change color, from 3 to 4 minutes. Add
  ½ cup dry sherry
  ¼ tsp each dried rosemary, sage, salt and black pepper
  3 sliced green onions
Stir gently until piping hot. Then toss with hot drained pasta. Taste and add more seasonings if needed.
*Makes: 2 servings*

*Fast Old-Fashioned Spaghetti*

# tips
# perfect pasta

The key to cooking great pasta is lots of water and cooking over high heat.

• For every pound of pasta, use 4 quarts (4L) of cold water in a very large pot. Once water comes to a full rolling boil, add 2 teaspoons salt. Wait for water to boil again. Then add all the pasta at one time. Immediately stir with a wooden spoon to keep pasta separated. Cook, uncovered, over high heat, stirring every few minutes.

• There's no need to add oil to the water. It will make noodles slippery, preventing a sauce from clinging.

• For al dente or "firm to the bite" consistency, dried pasta takes 7 to 12 minutes to cook; fresh pasta, 1 to 4 minutes.

• Remember that because the water is extremely hot, pasta will continue cooking while being drained. As soon as pasta is almost cooked, pour it into a colander.

• Do not rinse with cold water if you are serving pasta hot. Shake the colander several times to make sure all water is drained off.

• Immediately transfer the pasta to a warm serving dish and coat it lightly with your favorite sauce. Or add pasta to the sauce in the pan and stir for a couple of minutes so the pasta will absorb a little of the sauce.

### Oriental No-Cook Pastas

Most of the pasta we buy in North America is made from ground wheat and water, or from wheat, eggs and water. But noodles made with rice or mung beans are common in Oriental cuisine and are becoming increasingly popular here.

• Rice vermicelli are thin noodles made from rice flour that don't require boiling. Simply cover with warm water to soften and add to stir-fries and soups.

• Cellophane noodles or bean threads are translucent noodles made from mung beans. They're smooth and gelatinous, and require only soaking in warm water to soften. They have little taste but will absorb the flavor of the sauce they're added to.

pasta

# roasts

From this gorgeous-looking *Classic Roast with Veggies* (see recipe page 70) to our Express Roast Chicken, this chapter capitalizes on simply roasting the bird in the oven with little fixings or basting required so there's no need to turn the bird or be on constant watch. The payoff, besides little preparation, is the aroma of the whole bird as it achieves golden perfection.

## Classic Roast with Veggies

Choose seasonal vegetables to tuck around the chicken, such as spring's fresh new potatoes, leeks and baby carrots. They'll pick up the marvellous roasting juices from the chicken.

**PREPARATION: 15 MINUTES**
**ROASTING: 1½ HOURS**

Preheat oven to 375°F (190°C). Place in a large roasting pan, legs tied together loosely
**3-lb (1.5-kg) whole roasting chicken, giblets removed**
Rub with
**1 tbsp room-temperature butter**
**¼ tsp each salt and freshly ground black pepper**
Roast, uncovered, basting occasionally, for 1 hour. Meanwhile, slice dark green portion from
**3 leeks**
Slice lengthwise, separating leaves. Wash under cold running water. After 1 hour roasting, scatter leeks around chicken, along with
**12 small new potatoes, about the size of golf balls**
**6 scrubbed slim carrots**
**1 onion, quartered**
Stir to coat with pan juices. (If vegetables are crowded transfer some to a baking pan. Drizzle with pan juices. Place in oven below chicken.) Continue roasting, stirring vegetables occasionally, until potatoes are tender, about 35 more minutes. Remove chicken to a cutting board, cover and let sit 5 minutes before carving.
*Makes: 4 servings*

## Express Roast Chicken

Roasting a whole chicken at a high temperature for 12 minutes per pound produces an incredibly moist chicken with crispy skin.

**PREPARATION: 10 MINUTES**
**ROASTING: 40 MINUTES   SITTING: 12 MINUTES**

Preheat oven to 450°F (230°C). Remove giblets and neck from
**3-lb (1.5-kg) whole roasting chicken**
Rub with
**butter or olive oil**
Liberally sprinkle with
**salt (preferably sea salt)**
Place on a foil-lined baking sheet with shallow sides or a roasting pan. Roast, uncovered, for 36 minutes. Turn the oven off, but leave the chicken in the oven for 12 minutes. The internal temperature of the bird should reach 180°F (82°C). Cubes of peeled squash and potatoes sliced in half will roast beautifully around the chicken.
*Makes: 2 to 4 servings*

12-MINUTE ROASTING RULE
Roast chicken at 450°F (230°C) for 12 minutes per pound. Turn oven off but leave chicken in oven for 12 minutes. A 4 lb (2 kg) bird will take 48 minutes and a 5 lb (2.5 kg) bird 1 hour, plus 12 minutes resting time.

NOTE
The fat that runs off the chicken may spatter and create smoke. Reduce this risk by using a deep spoon or bulb baster to remove fat collected in the pan after about 20 minutes of roasting.

## Spring Roast with Rice

Freshly cut dill and tangy lemon add flavor to a gorgeous-looking, moist rice stuffing.

**PREPARATION: 20 MINUTES**
COOKING: 17 MINUTES
ROASTING: 1⅓ HOURS

In a medium-size saucepan over medium heat, melt
1 tbsp butter
Add
1½ cups long-grain rice
Stir for 2 minutes. Pour in and bring to a boil
2½ cups chicken broth or bouillon
1 tsp salt
Cover, reduce heat to low and cook for 10 minutes. Stir in
1 sliced carrot
Cover and continue cooking just until broth is absorbed, about 5 more minutes. Rice grains should still be firm. Then stir in
grated peel of 1 lemon
2 tbsp freshly squeezed lemon juice
1 chopped celery stalk
1 cup frozen peas
2 thinly sliced green onions
¼ cup chopped fresh dill
Preheat oven to 375°F (190°C). Remove giblets from
3-lb (1.5-kg) whole roasting chicken
Spoon stuffing loosely into breast and neck cavities. Fold skin over stuffing and secure with a skewer. Place remaining stuffing in a buttered baking dish and cover. Tie chicken legs together loosely. Place chicken in a roasting pan. Roast, uncovered, for 40 minutes. Baste with pan juices and place covered stuffing dish in oven.

Roast together, basting chicken often with pan juices, until a leg moves easily when wiggled, from 40 to 50 more minutes. Remove both from oven. Scoop stuffing from chicken. Stir into stuffing in dish along with
2 tbsp chopped fresh dill
Loosely cover chicken. Let sit 5 minutes before carving.
*Makes: 4 servings*

## Lemon-Rosemary Chicken

A little rosemary and thyme give tremendous character to a succulent bird.

**PREPARATION: 10 MINUTES**
ROASTING: 1¼ HOURS

Preheat oven to 375°F (190°C). In a small bowl, mix together
1 tsp dried rosemary, crumbled
½ tsp each dried leaf thyme, rubbed sage and cracked black pepper
¼ tsp celery salt
Remove giblets from
3½-lb (1.75-kg) whole roasting chicken
Inside the cavity, sprinkle a little of the rosemary mixture and
4 whole unpeeled garlic cloves
Tie legs together loosely and lightly butter or oil chicken skin. Squeeze over chicken
juice of half a lemon
Sprinkle remaining seasoning mixture evenly over chicken. Roast, uncovered, for 1¼ hours or 20 minutes per pound. Baste occasionally. Let chicken sit for 15 minutes before carving.
*Makes: 4 servings*

roasts

## Roast Chicken with Fresh Thyme

Aromatic thyme, onion and garlic spread under the chicken skin permeate the meat as it roasts to golden perfection.

**PREPARATION: 15 MINUTES**
**ROASTING: 1½ HOURS**

Preheat oven to 375°F (190°C). Using a fork, mix

- **2 tbsp room-temperature butter**
- **1 finely chopped small onion**
- **1 minced garlic clove**
- **2 tbsp finely chopped fresh thyme or 1 tsp dried thyme**
- **¼ tsp each salt and black pepper**

Remove giblets from

- **3½-lb (1.75-kg) whole roasting chicken**

Gently force skin away from breasts, then legs, by working your index finger between skin and flesh, starting at large cavity opening. Force about a quarter of butter mixture into each breast, between skin and meat, then push into legs. It will look lumpy. Force remaining butter mixture into each breast. Using your fingers on outside of skin, gently smooth butter mixture beneath so it covers most of each breast and leg. Tie legs together loosely. Place in a roasting pan. Roast, uncovered, for 30 minutes. Scatter around chicken

- **4 baking potatoes, cut lengthwise into 1-inch (2.5-cm) wedges**

Stir to coat with pan juices. Continue roasting, basting chicken and stirring potatoes every 15 minutes, until both are golden, 45 to 55 more minutes. Remove chicken to a cutting board and let sit 5 minutes before carving.
*Makes: 4 servings*

VARIATIONS
*Savory Sage*: Use 1 tsp dried rubbed sage in place of thyme in butter mixture.
*Garlic-Tarragon*: Use 1 tsp dried tarragon in place of thyme in butter mixture and increase garlic to 2 minced garlic cloves.

## Caribbean Mango-Rum Chicken

Flavored with curry, mango and cayenne for a little "island" heat, this is far from everyday ho-hum roast chicken. Serve with rice and peas and coleslaw for a tastebud-arousing Caribbean feast.

**PREPARATION: 10 MINUTES**
**ROASTING: 1½ HOURS**
**COOKING: 5 MINUTES**

Preheat oven to 375°F (190°C). Remove giblets from

- **3-lb (1.5-kg) whole roasting chicken**

Sprinkle over chicken and then rub into skin

- **1 tsp each poultry seasoning and curry powder**
- **¼ tsp cayenne (optional)**

Tie legs together loosely. Place in a roasting pan. Roast, uncovered, for 1 hour. Then pour over chicken

- **¼ cup mango nectar**

Continue roasting, basting with pan juices every 15 minutes, until chicken is golden and a drumstick moves easily, about 30 more minutes. Remove chicken to a heated platter. Pour juices into a measuring cup. Skim off and discard fat. Pour juices back into pan. Set roasting pan over medium heat. Add

- **¾ cup mango nectar**

Stir up any brown bits from bottom of pan while bringing to a boil. Stir in

- **2 tbsp chutney**
- **1 tbsp rum**

Serve sauce with slices of chicken.
*Makes: 4 servings*

SHOPPING TIP
Mango nectar is sold in individual-size fruit juice bottles where orange and other fruit juice drinks are sold.

# Roast Chicken with Caesar-Bacon Stuffing

Here's a homemade bread stuffing infused with all the great-tasting ingredients in a classic Caesar salad. It doesn't get much better than this.

**PREPARATION: 20 MINUTES**

**COOKING: 15 MINUTES    ROASTING: 1⅓ HOURS**

Preheat oven to 375°F (190°C). Remove giblets from
   **3½-lb (1.75-kg) whole roasting chicken**
In a frying pan, cook until crisp
   **4 slices bacon**
Drain on paper towels. Set aside 1 tbsp bacon fat. To remaining fat in pan add
   **2 tbsp olive oil**
   **1 chopped onion**
   **4 minced garlic cloves**
Sauté until softened, about 5 minutes. Remove from heat. Toast, then cut into cubes
   **5 slices regular white bread**
Place in a large bowl. Add onion mixture. Crumble in bacon. Stir in
   **½ tsp Worcestershire**
   **1 tsp finely grated lemon peel**
   **½ tsp each dry mustard and granulated sugar**
   **¼ tsp each salt and freshly ground black pepper**
   **½ cup freshly grated Parmesan**

Spoon some of the stuffing loosely into breast and neck cavities. Fold skin flaps over stuffing and secure with a small skewer. Place remaining stuffing in a buttered baking dish and cover. Tie legs together loosely. Place chicken in a roasting pan. Rub skin with reserved bacon fat. Roast, uncovered, for 40 minutes. Baste with pan juices. Place dish of stuffing in oven. Roast both together, basting chicken occasionally with pan juices, until a leg will move easily, from 40 to 50 more minutes. Remove stuffing and chicken from oven. Scoop stuffing from chicken breast and neck and stir into drier stuffing in baking dish. Stir in
   **½ cup chopped fresh parsley**
Loosely cover chicken. After chicken has sat 5 minutes, carve and serve with stuffing. The pan juices are delicious drizzled over chicken.
*Makes: 4 servings*

Roast Chicken with Caesar-Bacon Stuffing

roasts

## Asian-Glazed Chicken

Once you've tried it, we know you'll come to treasure this dynamite three-ingredient Oriental sauce – a beautiful contrast to the mild chicken it enhances.

**PREPARATION: 5 MINUTES**
**ROASTING: 50 MINUTES**

Preheat oven to 350°F (180°C). In a 9x13-inch (3-L) baking dish, place, bone-side up
  **6 skinless, bone-in chicken breasts or legs or 12 thighs**
In a small bowl, stir together
  **¼ cup teriyaki sauce**
  **1 tbsp sesame oil, preferably dark**
  **1 tbsp garlic-chili sauce or Sambal Oelek**
Brush a little over chicken. Roast, uncovered, 30 minutes. Turn chicken and generously brush with sauce. Continue roasting, basting with remaining sauce or pan juices, until chicken feels springy, about 20 minutes more for small or 40 minutes for larger pieces. Pan juices are terrific over chicken, as a dipping sauce or stirred into rice.
*Makes: 4 to 6 servings*

NOTE
*Sambal Oelek* is a paste made from fresh chilies, vinegar and salt. It's used in Indonesian cuisine as we use Tabasco, but beware, it's much hotter. It's sold in the Oriental section of supermarkets and in Chinese markets.

## Roast Chicken & Spicy Oven Fries

A salad dressing baste in this recipe gives great background taste to herbed chicken.

**PREPARATION: 15 MINUTES**
**ROASTING: 55 MINUTES**

Place one oven rack on lowest level and another in centre of oven. Preheat oven to 400°F (200°C). Stir together
  **⅓ cup Italian salad dressing**
  **½ to 1 tsp dried herbs, such as poultry seasoning, rosemary, Italian seasoning or oregano**
Place, bone-side up, in a large broiler pan
  **8 bone-in chicken legs or breasts**
Brush with about half of dressing mixture. In a large bowl, toss together
  **4 to 6 large potatoes, sliced into thick fries**
  **2 tbsp vegetable or olive oil**
  **½ tsp each crumbled dried parsley, garlic powder and salt**
  **¼ tsp each paprika and black pepper**
Spread on a baking sheet and place on lower rack. Place chicken on middle rack and roast for 20 minutes. Turn chicken and brush with remaining dressing. Stir potatoes. Continue roasting, until golden, from 35 to 45 more minutes. Baste chicken occasionally with pan juices.
*Makes: 4 servings*

## Honey-Lime Chicken

Tangy lime contrasts with salty soy sauce and sweet honey to produce a finger-licking sauce
so highly flavored that it works beautifully on low-fat skinless chicken.

**PREPARATION: 15 MINUTES**

**ROASTING: 1 HOUR**

Preheat oven to 350°F (180°C). In a 9x13-inch
(3-L) baking dish or dish with shallow sides,
place, bone-side up
**6 skinless, bone-in chicken pieces,
such as breasts, legs or thighs**
In a small bowl, stir together
**grated peel of 1 lime
freshly squeezed juice of 1 lime
¼ cup liquid honey
2 tbsp soy sauce
2 tsp each ground cumin and coriander
1 finely chopped small onion
1 minced large garlic clove**

Spoon sauce over chicken. Roast, uncovered,
30 minutes. Turn chicken bone-side down in
pan and continue roasting, basting often,
until chicken feels springy, from 30 to 45
more minutes. Lift chicken from juices. Skim
off and discard fat from juices, then use as a
dipping sauce or spoon over rice. Add a
mango salad and dinner is complete.
*Makes: 6 servings*

VARIATION
*Honey-Lemon:* Use grated peel and juice of
1 lemon in place of lime.

**roasts**

*Honey-Lime Chicken*

## Curried Apples & Chicken

This is not your typical curried chicken. Honey-glazed chicken pieces roast above curried apple wedges. Crank up the rice cooker to capture every last drop of the curried fruit sauce.

**PREPARATION: 15 MINUTES**
**ROASTING: 1 HOUR**

Preheat oven to 375°F (190°C). In a bowl, stir together
- **4 unpeeled baking apples, such as Granny Smith, cut into thin slices**
- **½ cup raisins**
- **2 tbsp freshly squeezed lemon juice**
- **2 tsp curry powder**

Scatter evenly over bottom of an oiled 9x13-inch (3-L) baking dish. Arrange, skin-side up, on top of apple mixture
- **4 large bone-in chicken breasts**

Sprinkle with
- **¼ tsp each salt and black pepper**

Stir together
- **¼ cup liquid honey**
- **1 tsp ground cumin**

Drizzle honey-cumin mixture over chicken. (Don't worry if it doesn't completely cover.) Roast, uncovered, 40 minutes. Then baste chicken with curried apple juices every 10 minutes, until chicken is springy, from 20 to 30 more minutes. If chicken becomes too brown, cover loosely with a tent of foil. Remove chicken. Stir into curried apples
- **2 sliced green onions**

Serve with the chicken. Add rice and dinner is complete.
*Makes: 4 to 6 servings*

## Speedy Chicken 'n' Stuffing

Use a stuffing mix and we guarantee you can quickly whip up a comfort dinner that tastes like it's made from scratch.

**PREPARATION: 15 MINUTES**
**COOKING: 10 MINUTES**
**ROASTING: 1 HOUR**

Preheat oven to 350°F (180°C). For a soft stuffing, butter an 8-inch (2-L) baking dish, or for a crunchy-topped stuffing, a 9x13-inch (3-L) dish. In a large saucepan over medium heat, melt
- **2 tbsp butter**

Add
- **1 chopped onion**
- **2 chopped celery stalks**
- **2 finely chopped carrots**

Stir often until onion has softened, about 5 minutes. Add and bring to a boil
- **1¼ cups water**

Then stir in until barely moist, sprinkling in the seasoning packet first, if there is one in the box
- **8-oz (227-g) box stuffing or 2 (4-oz/120-g) boxes stuffing mix**

Spread out stuffing in baking dish. Stir together
- **1 tbsp room-temperature butter**
- **¼ tsp poultry seasoning**

Rub over skin side of
- **4 large bone-in chicken breasts (skin removed if you wish)**

Arrange chicken, bone-side down, on top of stuffing. Roast, uncovered, until stuffing is browned and chicken feels springy, about 1 hour.
*Makes: 4 servings*

# Fire-Alarm Chicken

This speedy number has proven a big hit with *Chatelaine* staff, both for its intense flavor and heat. It cries out for cold beer.

**PREPARATION: 10 MINUTES**
**ROASTING: 50 MINUTES**

Preheat oven to 425°F (220°C). In a greased 9x13-inch (3-L) baking dish or a large baking sheet with shallow sides, place, skin-side up
**2 chicken halves or 6 pieces bone-in chicken**
Stir together
**2 tbsp olive oil**
**2 tsp hot red pepper flakes**
**½ tsp salt**
**¼ tsp cayenne**
Evenly rub over chicken skin. Then turn bone-side up. Roast, uncovered, for 30 minutes.

Turn chicken, skin-side up, and squeeze over top
**1 large lemon, sliced in half**
Continue roasting, basting with pan juices every 10 minutes, until chicken feels springy, from 20 to 30 more minutes. Lift chicken from juices. Skim off and discard fat from juices. Serve juices as a dipping sauce with chicken. Wonderful with stir-fried vegetables.
*Makes: 3 to 4 servings*

roasts

*Fire-Alarm Chicken*

roasts

## Chèvre & Sun-Dried Tomato Stuffed Breasts

This stuffed chicken from Toronto entrepreneur Philip Greey has an incredibly crispy skin and a luscious chèvre flavor comprised of only three ingredients.

**PREPARATION: 10 MINUTES**
**ROASTING: 50 MINUTES**

Preheat oven to 375°F (190°C). Drain
**½ cup oil-packed sun-dried tomatoes**
Save 1 tablespoon of the oil. Finely chop tomatoes and stir into
**4.5-oz (140-g) roll goat cheese**
**or ½ (8-oz/250-g) pkg cream cheese**
Using your fingers, tuck a rounded tablespoon of cheese mixture between skin and meat of
**8 bone-in chicken breasts with generous skin cover**
Push cheese mixture to centre of breast. Using your palm, gently press down on chicken skin until cheese is evenly distributed under skin. Then rub a little more of cheese mixture onto skin. Place breasts, skin-side up, on a 9x13-inch (3-L) baking dish. Drizzle with 1 tablespoon oil from tomatoes, then use your fingers to spread evenly over skin. Roast, basting occasionally with pan juices, until skin is golden and chicken feels springy, from 50 to 60 minutes. Skim fat from pan juices and discard. Drizzle pan juices over chicken.
*Makes: 6 to 8 servings*

VARIATIONS

For a change from sun-dried tomatoes with chèvre, try one of the following variations. For each, drizzle chicken with 1 tbsp olive oil in place of sun-dried tomato oil.

*Pesto:* Stir ½ cup chopped fresh basil and ¼ cup grated Parmesan into chèvre in place of tomatoes.

*Savory Cranberry:* Measure out ¼ cup dried cranberries. Finely chop. Stir into chèvre with ½ tsp poultry seasoning in place of tomatoes.

*Double Pepper:* Stir 1 tsp each coarsely ground black pepper and hot red pepper flakes into chèvre in place of tomatoes.

*Creamy Caesar:* Stir ¼ cup freshly grated Parmesan into ¼ cup creamy Caesar dressing. Use 1 tbsp in each breast in place of cheese-tomato mixture.

# Roasted Honey-Citrus Chicken

Oranges and lemons provide the zing in this recipe dedicated to chicken skin lovers.

**PREPARATION: 10 MINUTES**   ROASTING: 1 HOUR

Preheat oven to 375°F (190°C). Place bone-side down in a large baking sheet lined with foil
   **4 large bone-in chicken breasts**
Brush with
   **2 tbsp olive oil**
Roast, basting occasionally, for 40 minutes. Meanwhile, in a bowl, stir together
   **⅓ cup liquid honey**
   **finely grated peel of 1 orange and 1 lemon**
   **2 tbsp freshly squeezed lemon juice**
   **½ tsp dried basil**
   **¼ tsp each salt and freshly ground white or black pepper**
After 40 minutes, spoon over chicken and reduce heat to 350°F (180°C). Roast, uncovered, basting occasionally, until juices run clear when chicken is pierced with a knife, about 20 more minutes.
*Makes: 4 servings*

**roasts**

## tips
# bird basics

### Chicken Chatter

When roasting a whole chicken, here are some choices. Opt for large roasters or capons because there's a better meat-to-bone ratio with lots of leftovers for recycling into other meals.

*Capon*: A capon is a well-fed rooster that is castrated when quite young and weighs from 4 lbs (2 kg) to a whopping 10 lbs (5 kg). It has a high proportion of juicy breast meat.

*Roaster:* A roasting chicken usually weighs between 2½ lbs (1.25 kg) and 5 lbs (2.5 kg) and has a higher fat content and more taste than smaller broiler-fryers, making it ideal for rotisserie cooking or succulent roasting.

*Broiler-Fryer*: Weighing up to 3½ lbs (1.75 kg), these younger birds are great for barbecuing.

### As the Roast Turns

• Get a juicier chicken by roasting with breastbone down and back up in air (the opposite of the way we usually place it in roasting pan). This position means juices collect in breast instead of bony back.

• To hold chicken upside down, prop up breast sides with crumbled foil or buy a V-shaped roasting rack.

• The downside of this method is that you have to turn a hot chicken after about 45 minutes of roasting to brown the breast. The best technique is to remove the roasting pan from the oven and place on counter. Protecting your hands with oven mitts or thick terry tea towels, pick up chicken with two hands and turn. Avoid puncturing skin. Return to oven to finish roasting.

• The internal temperature of the bird should reach 180°F (82°C).

# salads

Move over mayonnaise and celery because popular salads are now dressed-up with fruit, curry and exotic vinaigrettes. This exciting *Thai Chicken Salad* (see recipe page 82) combines oranges, bean sprouts and a peanut dressing. Also check out a mango salad, a lusty Caesar, even a South Seas toss. Dig out your salad tongs.

## Thai Chicken Salad

Everyday ingredients create a salad that would be a winner in any Thai or Indonesian restaurant.

**PREPARATION: 15 MINUTES**
**COOKING: 9 MINUTES**

Place between two pieces of plastic wrap and flatten slightly by pounding with a heavy frying pan
  **4 skinless, boneless chicken breasts**
In a large nonstick frying pan over medium, heat
  **2 tsp vegetable or peanut oil**
Add chicken. Sauté until chicken feels springy, from 4 to 7 minutes per side. Remove and sprinkle with
  **salt and freshly ground pepper**
Refrigerate until cool.
In the same pan, heat
  **1 tsp sesame oil**
  **1 thinly julienned large carrot**
  **1 julienned large red pepper**
Stir-fry until vegetables are hot but still very crisp, about 1 minute. Turn onto a plate. (Chicken and julienned vegetables can be covered and refrigerated for up to 1 day.)
Add to vegetables
  **1 cup bean sprouts**
  **2 thinly sliced green onions**
Cut chicken into ½-inch (1-cm) wide slices and toss with vegetables. Then over a platter or individual dinner plates, scatter
  **1 head leafy lettuce, torn into bite-size pieces**
Arrange vegetables and chicken on top. Drizzle with
  **½ cup peanut dressing or sauce**
Arrange on top
  **1 orange, peeled and thinly sliced**
Sprinkle with
  **chopped coriander (optional)**
  *Makes: 4 servings*

## Great Chicken Caesar

Caesar tops restaurant salad sales, and ours tops that in flavor and nutrition.

**PREPARATION: 10 MINUTES**

In a large bowl, toss
  **1 lb (500 g) sliced roasted chicken breast, sliced into ½-inch (1-cm) strips, or 3 cups cubed cooked chicken or smoked chicken or turkey**
  **1 large head romaine lettuce, torn into bite-size pieces**
  **1 large julienned yellow, orange or red bell pepper**
Refrigerate if not using right away. When ready to serve, toss with
  **½ cup light creamy Caesar dressing**
Taste and add more dressing if needed. Sprinkle with
  **freshly ground black pepper**
  **½ cup freshly grated Parmesan**
  **2 cups croutons**
Serve right away with a crusty baguette and a glass of Beaujolais.
  *Makes: 4 servings*

# Chicken & Mango Party Salad

A honey-lime dressing adds a whimsical touch to this exceptionally sophisticated colorful salad.

**PREPARATION: 15 MINUTES**

In a small bowl, whisk together
**½ cup mayonnaise**
**¼ cup sour cream**
**1 tsp liquid honey**
**1 tbsp finely minced fresh ginger**
**finely grated peel of 1 lime**
**1 to 2 tbsp freshly squeezed lime juice**
Use right away or cover and refrigerate until ready to use. Dressing will keep well for about 3 days. Just before serving, prepare salad. Using a melon baller, scoop into balls
**1 cantaloupe**

Place in a medium-size bowl. Add and stir gently
**2 cups cubed cooked chicken**
**1 pint strawberries, sliced in half**
**1 large ripe mango, sliced**
**1 cup seedless green grapes**
**½ cup thinly sliced celery**
Line 4 dinner plates with
**whole leaves of Bibb or Boston lettuce**
Top with chicken-fruit mixture. Drizzle with dressing.
*Makes: 4 servings*

**salads**

*Chicken & Mango Party Salad*

salads

## Chicken Salad with Gorgonzola

Chunks of creamy Gorgonzola and sweet peppers make this a wonderfully impressive weekend-entertaining lunch.

**PREPARATION: 15 MINUTES**

Arrange on serving plates or in a large salad bowl
  **1 small head Boston or leaf lettuce,
      torn into bite-size pieces**
Top with
  **2 cups coarsely chopped cooked chicken**
  **2 julienned carrots**
  **1 thinly sliced sweet red pepper**
  **¼ cup crumbled Gorgonzola, Stilton
      or other blue cheese**
Whisk together
  **2 tbsp each olive oil, orange juice
      concentrate and water**
  **¼ tsp salt**
  **pinches of cayenne and black pepper**
Drizzle dressing over salad. Garnish with fresh orange slices if you wish. Serve immediately.
*Makes: 2 to 4 servings*

## Curried Chicken Salad

It takes mere minutes to create a creamy dressing bursting with flavor, not fat.

**PREPARATION: 10 MINUTES**

In a small bowl, stir together
  **¼ cup sour cream**
  **2 tbsp mayonnaise**
  **1 tbsp freshly squeezed lime juice**
  **1 tsp curry powder**
  **½ tsp each chili powder and ground cumin**
  **¼ tsp ground ginger**
  **pinch of salt and freshly ground black pepper**
Set aside. Covered and refrigerated, dressing will keep well for 2 to 3 days.

In a large bowl, mix
  **6 cooked chicken breasts,
      cut into 1-inch (2.5-cm) pieces**
  **1 peeled apple, diced**
  **3 thinly sliced celery stalks**
Stir in dressing until chicken is evenly coated. At this point, chicken mixture can be covered and refrigerated overnight if you wish. When ready to serve, line 4 salad plates with **whole leaves of Boston lettuce**
Spoon chicken mixture onto lettuce and serve immediately.
*Makes: 4 servings*

## South Seas Chicken Salad

Upscale preserved ginger gives a unique twist to this island salad.

**PREPARATION: 15 MINUTES**

In a small bowl, whisk together until well blended
  **¼ cup vegetable oil**
  **2 tbsp finely chopped preserved ginger**
  **1 tbsp orange juice concentrate**
  **finely grated peel of 1 orange**
  **pinch of salt and black pepper**
Set aside. Covered and refrigerated, dressing will keep well for about a week. Chop and combine in a bowl
  **4 cooked skinless, boneless chicken breasts**
  **½ small English cucumber**
  **1 sweet red pepper**
  **1 ripe mango, peeled**
Toss with enough dressing to moisten. Taste and add more chopped ginger, salt or pepper if needed. Line a platter with **whole leafy lettuce leaves**
Spoon chicken mixture on top of lettuce. Sprinkle with
  **2 tbsp toasted pine nuts or chopped roasted peanuts**
*Makes: 4 servings*

# East Meets West Noodle Salad

This Oriental-inspired salad is great for a picnic buffet or a formal party.
And it's proof that "reduced fat" needn't mean boring!

**PREPARATION: 30 MINUTES**

**COOKING: 15 MINUTES**

salads

In a large pot of boiling salted water, cook until al dente, about 8 minutes
    **1-lb (450-g) pkg spaghetti**
Drain well. Immediately toss in a large mixing bowl with
    **2 tsp sesame oil**
Stir together, then stir into pasta
    **finely grated peel of 1 lime**
    **¼ cup freshly squeezed lime juice**
    **2 tbsp soy sauce**
    **2 tsp Oriental chili-garlic sauce
        or Sambal Oelek (see note page 74)**
    **1 tsp each salt and sugar**
Set aside. Then slice into bite-size pieces
    **4 skinless, boneless chicken breasts**
In a large frying pan over medium-high, heat
    **2 tbsp vegetable oil**
Add about half the chicken and stir until golden, about 3 minutes. Remove from pan. Repeat with remaining chicken.

Return chicken plus juices to pan. Add
    **2 minced garlic cloves**
    **1 thinly sliced onion**
Stir until onion has softened, about 3 minutes. Add
    **¼ cup water**
    **2 thinly julienned carrots**
    **1 julienned red pepper**
    **4 thinly sliced celery stalks**
Stir often for 3 minutes. Add
    **¼ lb (125 g) snow peas, trimmed**
Stir until bright green, about 1 minute. Toss with spaghetti and
    **½ cup finely chopped fresh coriander**
    **4 thinly sliced green onions**
Serve right away. Or if taking to a picnic, refrigerate, uncovered, for up to a day. Salad is good warm, at room temperature or chilled.
*Makes: 4 to 6 servings*

## tips

## salad days

**Leftover chicken is perfect for salad. Here's some great combos to try:**

• **Add grated lime and orange zest to mayonnaise along with lime juice. Toss with chopped chicken, diced mango, red pepper and jalapeño peppers. Add a sprinkle of toasted coconut and fresh coriander.**

• **Toss chopped chicken with Caesar dressing. Add chopped celery, green onions, crisp crumbled bacon and Parmesan.**

• **Toss chicken with mayonnaise jazzed up with grated lemon peel and juice or curry powder or paste. Add chopped apples, chopped celery and toasted pecans.**

• **Make a vinaigrette with a little sesame oil, rice wine vinegar, ginger and hot garlic-chili sauce. Add chopped chicken, green onions, chopped water chestnuts and blanched snow peas.**

# sauces
## and salsas

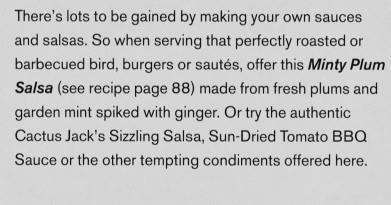

There's lots to be gained by making your own sauces and salsas. So when serving that perfectly roasted or barbecued bird, burgers or sautés, offer this *Minty Plum Salsa* (see recipe page 88) made from fresh plums and garden mint spiked with ginger. Or try the authentic Cactus Jack's Sizzling Salsa, Sun-Dried Tomato BBQ Sauce or the other tempting condiments offered here.

## Minty Plum Salsa

You'll want to eat this fruit mélange by the bowlful, but spoon it lavishly instead over grilled chicken burgers or serve with breasts.

**PREPARATION: 20 MINUTES**
**REFRIGERATION: 1 HOUR**

In a medium-size bowl, combine
  1 lb (500 g) purple plums,
    about 6 large plums, diced
  finely grated peel of 1 lime or lemon
  2 tsp freshly squeezed lime or lemon juice
Toss well. Add
  1 finely chopped red onion
  1 finely chopped small hot banana pepper
  ¼ bunch finely chopped parsley sprigs,
    about ½ cup
  ½ bunch finely chopped fresh mint leaves,
    about ¼ cup
  2 tbsp olive oil
  1 tsp grated fresh ginger
  generous pinch of salt
Toss with plum mixture. Refrigerate for about
  1 hour to give flavors a chance to develop.
  Taste and add up to 1 tablespoon sugar if
  needed. Cover and refrigerate for up to 3 days.
  *Makes: 3 cups*

## Incredibly Fast Salsa

Dress up salsa and add instant flavor to chicken burgers with this really easy recipe. Perfect for Parmesan Italian Burgers (see recipe page 37).

**PREPARATION: 5 MINUTES**

Stir together
  2 finely chopped seeded ripe tomatoes
  ¼ cup bottled salsa, medium or hot
Use right away or leave at room temperature for
  1 hour.
  *Makes: 1⅓ cups*

## Quick Stir-Together Peanut Sauce

Chicken loves to be dipped into peanut sauce. Whip up this homemade version, far superior to store-bought, in just 15 minutes.

**PREPARATION: 15 MINUTES**

In a medium-size bowl, stir together
  ½ cup peanut butter
  1 minced small garlic clove
  2 tbsp soy sauce
  juice of 1 lime
  1 tsp granulated sugar
  ½ tsp ground ginger
  ¼ tsp each cayenne and salt
Whisk in
  ¼ cup boiling water
Then stir in
  ¼ cup chopped fresh coriander
Covered and refrigerated, sauce will keep well
  for several days. (If peanut sauce becomes
  thick, thin by whisking in hot water
  1 tablespoon at a time, or warm in microwave.)
  *Makes: ¾ cup*

## Spicy Mango-Salsa Sauce

This salsa adds pizzazz to the simplest chicken sauté or roast chicken.

**PREPARATION: 10 MINUTES**

In a bowl, stir together
  2 chopped ripe mangoes
  juice of 1 lime
  1 tbsp brown sugar
  ¼ to ½ tsp hot pepper sauce
  ½ cup chopped fresh coriander
Let stand at room temperature for about 1 hour
  or cover and refrigerate for up to 1 day. When
  ready to serve, stir in
  2 thinly sliced green onions
  *Makes: 1 cup*

## Garlicky Spread

The advantage of this special garlic spread over garlic butter is that it's lower in cholesterol and spreadable right out of the refrigerator.

**PREPARATION: 5 MINUTES**

Stir together
- ½ cup room-temperature butter
- ½ cup olive or vegetable oil
- 2 to 4 minced large garlic cloves
- 2 tbsp finely chopped parsley

The oil keeps this spread soft enough to easily brush on chicken before putting on the grill. Store in the refrigerator. It will keep for at least a week and also freezes well. It's great on vegetables and bread.

*Makes: 1 cup*

## Refrigerator Stir-Fry Sauce

With a jar of this sauce, you always have the basis for a quick dinner.

**PREPARATION: 5 MINUTES**

In a jar with a tight-fitting lid, place
- ¾ cup light soy sauce
- ½ cup chicken broth or bouillon
- ¼ cup dry sherry or 3 tbsp ketchup
- 3 tbsp brown sugar
- ¼ cup cornstarch
- 4 minced garlic cloves
- 2 tbsp chopped fresh ginger
  or 1 tsp ground ginger

Seal and shake to combine ingredients. Refrigerate until ready to use. Sauce will keep for several days. Shake well before adding from ¼ to ½ cup to a stir-fry.

*Makes: 1⅓ cups*

**sauces and salsas**

*Incredibly Fast Salsa*

sauces and salsas

## Cactus Jack's Sizzling Salsa

Cactus Jack's, a cozy diner in Carmel, California, makes an incredible salsa. Here it's trimmed down so you can enjoy it too.

**PREPARATION: 15 MINUTES**
COOKING: 15 MINUTES

In a large wide saucepan, place
  **2 (28-oz) cans diced tomatoes, including juice**
  **¼ tsp salt**
  or
  **6 cups coarsely chopped peeled ripe tomatoes**
  **7½-oz can tomato sauce**
  **½ tsp salt**
To either tomato base, add
  **4 chopped seeded jalapeños or 4-oz (114-ml) can drained chopped green chilies**
  **6 minced garlic cloves**
  **1 tbsp each paprika and ground cumin**
Place over high heat and bring to a boil, stirring often. Reduce heat to medium-low and boil gently, uncovered, stirring often, for 10 minutes. Stir into mixture
  **2 finely chopped onions**
  **¼ cup finely chopped fresh coriander**
Continue cooking, stirring often, until most of liquid has evaporated, about 5 to 10 more minutes. Stir frequently, especially near end of cooking time. Remove salsa from heat. Stir in
  **¼ cup finely chopped fresh coriander**
  **3 tbsp freshly squeezed lime juice**
Taste and add more lime juice if you like. Store salsa in a sealed jar in the refrigerator. Salsa will keep well for up to a week and can be frozen. Serve with crisp tortilla chips for dipping, or use in Fast Spicy Mexican Lasagna (see recipe page 56). When freezing salsa, be sure to leave at least 1-inch (2.5-cm) headspace in the containers as salsa expands when it freezes.
*Makes: 7 cups*

## Sun-Dried Tomato BBQ Sauce

This robust sauce's character comes from sun-dried tomatoes and balsamic vinegar.

**PREPARATION: 15 MINUTES**
COOKING: 20 MINUTES

In a food processor, whirl, using an on-and-off motion, until coarsely chopped
  **1 onion, quartered**
  **1 green pepper, quartered**
  **8 sun-dried tomatoes**
  **2 garlic cloves**
Add
  **19-oz can drained whole tomatoes**
Whirl just until coarsely chopped. Pour into a saucepan and add
  **¼ cup brown sugar**
  **2 tbsp balsamic vinegar**
  **3 tbsp tomato paste**
Bring to a boil, stirring until sugar is dissolved. Reduce heat and simmer gently, covered, stirring often, about 10 minutes. Uncover and simmer for about 10 minutes to thicken. Wonderful served with roasted or grilled chicken, spooned on chicken burgers or fajitas, or as a dipping sauce with kebabs.
*Makes: 2½ cups*

## Oriental BBQ Sauce

The combined sweet-and-sour flavors with fresh ginger permeate this Asian baste that's terrific on any cut of chicken or as a dipping sauce.

**PREPARATION: 15 MINUTES**
**COOKING: 10 MINUTES**

In a medium-size saucepan over medium, heat
   **1 tbsp peanut or vegetable oil**
Add
   **1 finely chopped onion**
   **1 finely chopped green pepper**
   **1 tbsp grated fresh ginger**
Cook, stirring often, until softened, about 5 minutes. Stir in
   **½ cup each ketchup and hoisin sauce**
   **2 tbsp vinegar**
Reduce heat to low. Cover and simmer to develop flavors, stirring often, about 5 minutes. Then stir in
   **3 thinly sliced green onions**
*Makes: 1½ cups*

## Mango & Avocado Salsa

A glamorous topper for grilled or chilled chicken. Make ahead, if you like, but add the avocado just before serving.

**PREPARATION: 20 MINUTES**
**REFRIGERATION: 1 HOUR**

In a medium-size bowl, combine
   **1 large mango, peeled and cut into**
      **¼-inch (0.5-cm) pieces**
   **1 finely chopped sweet red pepper**
   **½ red onion, finely chopped**
   **⅓ cup snipped chives**
   **2 tbsp olive oil**
   **1 tbsp freshly squeezed lemon or lime juice**
   **pinch of salt**
   **1 large avocado, diced**
Toss ingredients. Taste and add a pinch of sugar or more lemon juice if you wish. Refrigerate for about 1 hour to give flavors a chance to develop. Salsa is best served the same day it is made.
*Makes: 3 cups*

**sauces and salsas**

## tips
## salsa savvy

• Use salsa on top of burgers. Or when making burgers, stir about ¼ cup salsa into 1 lb (500 g) regular ground chicken along with 1 egg and ½ cup store-bought fine dry bread crumbs. Salsa is also wonderful on top of grilled chicken pieces, steaks, grilled cheese sandwiches, even scrambled eggs.

• Combine ¼ cup salsa and ¼ cup white wine in a frying pan. Then simmer skinless, boneless chicken breasts in salsa mixture.

• Roast skinless, bone-in chicken breasts at 350°F (180°C) for 30 minutes. Top with salsa sauce, then grated Parmesan or cheddar. Continue roasting for 20 to 30 more minutes.

# sautés

A sauté is a swift in-and-out of the frying pan technique perfectly suited to boneless chicken breasts and budget-priced thighs. For a classy number that's special enough for company, consider this **French Bistro Chicken** (see recipe page 94) flavored with shallots and vermouth.

sautés

## French Bistro Chicken

Tender, golden chicken breasts seasoned with herbs are simmered in a vermouth-laced sauce in this unpretentious recipe.

**PREPARATION: 10 MINUTES**
COOKING: 18 MINUTES

In a large frying pan over medium-high, melt
**1 tbsp butter**
Add
**4 small or 2 large skinless, boneless chicken breasts**
Sauté until golden, from 3 to 5 minutes per side. Remove to a plate. Reduce heat to medium. Add
**1 tbsp butter**
**¼ cup finely chopped shallots**
Stir often, until softened, about 4 minutes. Push to side of pan and return chicken, plus any juices on plate, to centre of pan. Sprinkle over chicken and shallots
**¼ tsp each dried tarragon, thyme, oregano, salt and pepper**
**juice of half a large lemon**
Add to pan
**⅓ cup dry vermouth or sherry**
Cover and cook for 5 minutes. Turn chicken, stir liquid and continue cooking, covered, from 3 to 5 minutes. Serve with new potatoes and asparagus.
*Makes: 2 servings*

## Chicken with Maple Syrup Glaze

White wine and maple syrup turn into a sublime glaze for chicken in this sophisticated entrée.

**PREPARATION: 10 MINUTES**
COOKING: 14 MINUTES

In a frying pan over medium, heat
**1 tsp butter**
Add
**4 skinless, boneless chicken breasts**
Sauté until golden, from 3 to 5 minutes per side. Add
**2 thinly sliced green onions**
**2 tbsp each white wine and maple syrup**
Cover, reduce heat to medium-low and simmer until chicken feels springy, from 8 to 10 more minutes. Turn partway through. Serve with maple-wine sauce poured over top. Terrific with squash or sweet potatoes.
*Makes: 4 servings*

## Saucy Basil-Balsamic Sauté

A drizzle of balsamic vinegar works just as well in this recipe as in a vinaigrette.

**PREPARATION: 10 MINUTES**
COOKING: 17 MINUTES

In a large frying pan over medium, melt
**1 tbsp butter**
Add
**4 skinless, boneless chicken breasts**
Sauté until golden, from 3 to 5 minutes per side. Add
**¼ cup chicken broth or bouillon**
**1 tbsp balsamic vinegar**
**¼ tsp dried leaf basil**
Cover, reduce heat to medium-low and simmer until chicken feels springy, from 8 to 10 minutes. Turn chicken partway through. Remove chicken. Increase heat to high. Then boil sauce, stirring often, until reduced to about ¼ cup, 3 to 5 minutes. Pour over breasts.
*Makes: 2 to 4 servings*

# Glamorous Chèvre-Stuffed Chicken

If you're in the mood for an upscale, but fast, entrée, this recipe will deliver. Perfect with an asparagus risotto.

**PREPARATION: 20 MINUTES**
**COOKING: 14 MINUTES**

In a small bowl, stir with a fork
  2 oil-packed sun-dried tomatoes, drained and finely chopped
  ¼ cup creamy goat cheese
  1 minced garlic clove
  ¼ tsp freshly ground black pepper

Using a paring knife, cut a slit or pocket, starting at the widest end, in each of
  4 skinless, boneless chicken breasts

Stuff one-quarter of cheese mixture into each breast. Stuff as close to centre of breasts as possible to prevent filling from oozing out during cooking. In a large frying pan over medium-low, heat
  1 tbsp vegetable oil

Add chicken. Cover and cook, turning once, until chicken feels springy, from 14 to 18 minutes.
*Makes: 4 servings*

# Puttanesca Chicken

Here's a smart way to an Italian classic. It's not only flavorful and rich, but low in fat.

**PREPARATION: 15 MINUTES**
**COOKING: 20 MINUTES**

In a wide saucepan over medium-high heat, place
  1 chopped large onion
  3 minced garlic cloves
    or 1 tsp bottled minced garlic
  ½ cup dry red wine

Cover and bring to a boil. Reduce heat and simmer, stirring often, for 5 minutes. Then stir in
  19-oz can drained plum tomatoes
  ¼ cup sliced black olives
  2 tsp anchovy paste
  1 to 2 tbsp capers

Into this sauce, submerge
  4 skinless, boneless chicken breasts

Cover and simmer, turning often, until chicken feels springy, from 12 to 15 minutes. If you prefer a thicker sauce, transfer chicken to a platter. Then boil sauce over high heat until thickened, about 3 minutes. Perfect over pasta or rice.
*Makes: 4 servings*

*French Bistro Chicken*

## Crispy Cornmeal-Chili Chicken

It takes a mere minute or two to add a
crunchy coating to chicken breasts that are
a real winner with kids.

**PREPARATION: 15 MINUTES**

**COOKING: 14 MINUTES**

In a pie plate, using a fork, stir together
  3 tbsp cornmeal
  1 tsp chili powder
  ¼ tsp cumin
  ⅛ tsp each salt and freshly ground black
    or cayenne pepper
Dip into cornmeal mixture
  4 skinless, boneless chicken breasts
Press into mixture to ensure a good coating on
  all sides. In a large frying pan over medium-
  low, heat
  1 tbsp vegetable oil
Add chicken. Sauté until golden and chicken
  feels springy, from 7 to 10 minutes per side.
  Serve heaped with salsa, tomato or chili sauce
  and oven-fried potato wedges.
*Makes: 4 servings*

## Elegant Chicken with Wine & Watercress

Watercress is a great addition to
this recipe, but taste before adding to sauce.
If bitter, add only 2 tablespoons.

**PREPARATION: 10 MINUTES**

**COOKING: 12 MINUTES**

In a large frying pan over medium, heat
  ½ tbsp olive or vegetable oil
When hot, add
  4 large skinless, boneless chicken breasts

Sauté, turning once, until well browned on
  both sides and springy, from 6 to 8 minutes
  per side. Add
  ½ cup white wine
  ¼ cup finely chopped watercress
  ¼ tsp each salt and freshly ground white
    pepper
Remove chicken to a serving platter and cover to
  keep warm. Add to sauce
  1 to 2 tbsp cold butter,
    cut into several pieces
Whisk sauce vigorously until blended. Pour over
  chicken and serve.
*Makes: 4 servings*

## Lemon-Sage Sauté

Want a fast rewarding dinner?
Serve this with broccoli and microwave baked
potatoes topped with sour cream.

**PREPARATION: 2 MINUTES**

**COOKING: 12 MINUTES**

In a wide frying pan over medium, heat
  1 tbsp olive oil
Add
  4 skinless, boneless chicken breasts
Evenly crumble over chicken, turning to coat
  both sides
  1 tsp dried rubbed sage
Sauté, covered, until chicken feels springy, from
  6 to 8 minutes per side. Sprinkle with
  pinch of salt
  generous grinding of black pepper
  juice of half a lemon
Remove from pan and serve.
*Makes: 4 servings*

# Terrific Teriyaki Sauté

Brimming with Oriental flavors, this is low-fat fare at its best.

**PREPARATION: 10 MINUTES**
**COOKING: 14 MINUTES**

In a large nonstick frying pan over medium, heat
  1 tsp sesame oil
Add
  4 skinless, boneless chicken breasts
Sauté until golden, about 5 minutes per side.
  Stir in
  2 tbsp each soy sauce and sherry
  1 tsp granulated sugar
  pinch of ground ginger
    or 1½ tsp finely chopped fresh ginger

Then add
  1 head broccoli, broken into small florets
  1 thinly sliced red pepper
Cover and simmer, turning vegetables and
  chicken partway through, until vegetables
  are done as you like, from 4 to 6 minutes.
  Serve on rice and sprinkle with
  3 thinly sliced green onions
  *Makes: 4 servings*

sautés

*Terrific Teriyaki Sauté*

## Oriental Ginger-Peanut Sauté

If you're in the mood for Thai, here's a five-ingredient route that takes only 20 minutes. Serve with stir-fried rice and veggies.

**PREPARATION: 10 MINUTES**
**COOKING: 15 MINUTES**

In a large frying pan over medium, heat
**1 tbsp peanut or vegetable oil**
Add
**4 skinless, boneless chicken breasts**
Cook, covered, turning once, until golden, from 12 to 14 minutes. Transfer to dinner plates. Cover to keep warm. Keeping pan off heat, stir in
**1 tsp grated fresh ginger
   or bottled minced ginger**
**2 sliced green onions**
Return pan to medium heat and stir mixture for 1 minute. Pour in
**¼ cup homemade peanut sauce (see recipe page 88) or store-bought peanut sauce**
**1 tbsp soy sauce**
When bubbling, drizzle over chicken. Top with
**chopped roasted peanuts or coriander sprigs (optional)**
*Makes: 4 servings*

## Garlic Chicken Provençal

The classic Provençal dish has 40, yes 40, cloves of garlic. This cheater's version delivers the same flavor return.

**PREPARATION: 10 MINUTES**
**COOKING: 20 MINUTES**

Flatten, using the fleshy side of your fist
**4 skinless, boneless chicken breasts**
In a large nonstick frying pan over medium-high, melt
**2 tsp butter**
Add chicken and sauté until lightly golden, about 3 minutes per side. Remove chicken from pan.

Stir in
**½ cup white wine**
**1 cup chicken broth or bouillon**
**1 tsp each dried tarragon and Dijon**
**4 large garlic cloves, each sliced lengthwise into 3 or 4 pieces**
Boil gently, uncovered, for 3 minutes. Then place chicken on top of garlic. Cover and simmer, turning chicken halfway through, until chicken feels springy, about 7 minutes. Remove chicken and cover to keep warm. Boil sauce over medium-high, uncovered, until reduced to about ½ cup, about 5 minutes. If you like, stir in
**¼ cup sour cream (optional)**
Terrific with noodles and steamed spinach.
*Makes: 4 servings*

## Caesar-Basil Chicken

Besides being one of our most fragrant summer herbs, basil has become as common as chives in backyard gardens across the country.

**PREPARATION: 10 MINUTES**
**COOKING: 14 MINUTES**

In a wide frying pan over medium-high, heat
**2 tsp olive oil**
Add
**2 to 3 skinless, boneless chicken breasts**
Sauté until golden, from 3 to 5 minutes per side. Reduce heat to medium-low and stir in
**2 chopped large tomatoes**
**¼ cup creamy Caesar dressing**
**¼ tsp hot pepper sauce or other hot sauce**
Cover and simmer, turning chicken once, until chicken feels springy, from 8 to 10 minutes. Stir in
**¼ cup coarsely chopped fresh basil**
**pinches of salt and black pepper**
Wonderful with mashed potatoes or rice and steamed green beans.
*Makes: 2 servings*

# Cumin-Cinnamon Chicken

A simple dusting of cumin and cinnamon
creates a very elegant flavoring for quick-cook chicken breasts. In 15 minutes,
you can have a touch of Morocco.

**PREPARATION: 5 MINUTES**
**COOKING: 12 MINUTES**

In a large frying pan over medium heat, melt
**1 tbsp butter or olive oil**
Add
**1 minced large garlic clove**
**4 skinless, boneless chicken breasts**
Sprinkle both sides of chicken evenly with
**½ tsp ground cumin or 1 tsp cumin seeds**
**⅛ tsp ground cinnamon**
**pinch of ground white pepper**

Sauté chicken, covered, from 6 to 8 minutes per
side. Serve with thin slices of gingered carrots.
*Makes: 4 servings*

**sautés**

*Cumin-Cinnamon Chicken*

**sautés**

## Jalapeño Cashew Chicken

A voluptuous party sauté from North 44°
in Toronto. Chef Mark McEwan's glamorous entrée
takes only 30 minutes from start to table.

**PREPARATION: 10 MINUTES**
**COOKING: 20 MINUTES**

In a saucepan, combine
- **10-oz can chicken broth**
- **2 tbsp balsamic vinegar**
- **1 tbsp finely chopped seeded jalapeño**
- **1 minced garlic clove**

Bring to a boil. Then reduce heat and simmer,
covered, for 4 minutes. Remove from heat.
In a small bowl, combine
- **2 tbsp olive oil**
- **1 tsp minced jalapeño**
- **1 minced garlic clove**
- **generous grinding of white pepper**

Brush over
- **6 large skinless, boneless chicken breasts**

In a wide frying pan over medium, heat
- **1 tbsp each butter and olive oil**

Add chicken and cook until golden, about
3 to 5 minutes per side. Then reduce heat
to low. Cook, covered, turning once, until
chicken feels springy, 5 more minutes. About
2 minutes before chicken is cooked, place
balsamic sauce over high heat.
Add one piece at a time
- **¼ cup cold butter, cut into 4 pieces**

Stir rapidly until completely incorporated
before adding the next piece, then stir in
- **½ cup toasted coarsely chopped cashews**

Remove from heat. Spoon over chicken on
warm plates.
*Makes: 6 servings*

## Chicken Sauté with Wild Mushrooms

A new take on chicken à la king, this updated
number lets Dijon, not cream, add taste.

**PREPARATION: 15 MINUTES**
**COOKING: 20 MINUTES**

In a large nonstick frying pan over medium-
high, heat
- **1 tbsp olive oil**

Add
- **4 skinless, boneless chicken breasts**

Sauté until golden, about 3 minutes per side.
Remove from pan. Add to oil in pan
- **½ lb (250 g) sliced mushrooms,**
  **such as shiitake, oyster, cremini or button,**
  **or a mixture (about 3 cups total)**

Stir often just until mushrooms release their
juices, about 4 minutes. Stir in
- **½ tsp Dijon**
- **¼ tsp each salt and freshly ground black pepper**

Measure out
- **1 cup white wine or chicken broth**

In a large measuring cup, whisk 2 tbsp of the
wine or chicken broth until smooth with
- **2 tbsp all-purpose flour**

While stirring constantly, slowly add remaining
white wine or chicken broth. Pour over
mushrooms and stir constantly over
medium-high, until thickened, about
5 minutes. Return chicken plus any juices
to pan. Cover and reduce heat to low.
Simmer until chicken feels springy, from 5 to
8 minutes. Turn breasts halfway through and
stir sauce occasionally. Serve on a bed of rice
sprinkled with green onions.
*Makes: 4 servings*

## Chicken Chèvre à Deux

When you've got chèvre leftover from a party,
put it to good use with this classy dish.

**PREPARATION: 5 MINUTES**
**COOKING: 13 MINUTES**

In a frying pan over medium, heat
**1 to 2 tsp olive oil or butter**
Add
**2 skinless, boneless chicken breasts**
Sauté until golden, about 5 minutes per side.
Place in centre of each breast
**1 tbsp herbed goat cheese**
Cover and cook until cheese is hot, about
3 minutes. If necessary, gently spread cheese
to cover breasts. Then sprinkle each with
**shredded fresh basil or generous pinches**
**of dried basil**
**coarsely ground black pepper**
*Makes: 2 servings*

## Marsala Chicken

This richly glazed chicken uses
a little marsala or sherry.

**PREPARATION: 5 MINUTES**
**COOKING: 18 MINUTES**

In a large frying pan over medium, melt
**1 tbsp butter**
Add
**4 skinless, boneless chicken breasts**
Sauté until golden, from 3 to 5 minutes per side.
Pour over chicken
**⅓ cup marsala or sweet sherry**
**½ tsp freshly squeezed lemon juice**
**pinches of salt and white pepper**
Cover, reduce heat to low and simmer until
chicken feels springy, from 4 to 5 minutes per
side. Remove chicken to a platter. Increase
heat to high. Boil marsala, uncovered and
stirring often, until reduced to about 2 tbsp.
Pour over breasts. Serve over noodles.
*Makes: 2 to 4 servings*

## Thyme-Dijon Chicken

This fast sauté is the perfect match for mashed
potatoes or a vegetable pilaf.

**PREPARATION: 15 MINUTES**
**COOKING: 18 MINUTES**

In a large frying pan over medium, heat
**1 tsp each vegetable oil and butter**
Add
**4 to 6 skinless, boneless chicken breasts**
**pinches of salt and pepper**
Sauté until golden, from 3 to 5 minutes per side.
Remove chicken to a plate. Add to pan
**¼ cup finely sliced shallots**
**¼ tsp dried leaf thyme**
Stir to remove brown bits from bottom. Stir
often for 2 minutes. Stir in until blended
**2 tsp Dijon**
**¼ cup dry white wine**
**¼ cup chicken broth or bouillon**
Return chicken plus any juices to pan. Cover and
bring to a boil. Then simmer over low heat,
turning chicken once, until chicken feels
springy, about 10 minutes. Remove to platter.
Stir into sauce
**¼ cup sour cream**
**pinches of salt and pepper**
Pour over chicken.
*Makes: 4 to 6 servings*

sautés

## Curried Coconut Chicken

Create a robust curry without numerous spices.
Here chicken is quickly braised in silken coconut
milk flavored with curry paste.

**PREPARATION: 15 MINUTES**
**COOKING: 25 MINUTES**

In a large wide saucepan, combine
   **14-oz (400-mL) can coconut milk**
   **2 tsp curry paste or powder**
Bring to a boil over medium heat, stirring until
   blended. When sauce comes to a boil, add
   **4 skinless, boneless chicken breasts**
      **or 8 thighs**
Cover and reduce heat to medium-low. Simmer
   for 10 minutes, turning chicken partway
   through. Remove to a plate. Add to sauce
   **½ small head cauliflower,**
      **broken into florets, about 5 cups**
   **1 julienned large red pepper**
Place chicken on top of vegetables. Cover and
   continue cooking until vegetables are almost
   done, from 5 to 7 minutes. Remove chicken
   and vegetables to a warm platter and cover.
   Increase heat to medium-high. Boil sauce,
   uncovered, stirring often, until thickened,
   about 8 minutes. Pour over chicken and
   vegetables. Serve over rice and sprinkle with
   shredded basil or coriander.
*Makes: 4 servings*

## Moroccan Tomato Sauté

Fresh mint gives a romantic edge to this
cumin-tomato sauce quickie.

**PREPARATION: 15 MINUTES**
**COOKING: 17 MINUTES**

In a large frying pan over medium, heat
   **1 tsp each butter and olive oil**
Add
   **4 small skinless, boneless chicken breasts**
      **or 6 to 8 thighs**
Sauté until golden, from 3 to 5 minutes per side.
   Push to edge of pan. Add to centre
   **1 finely chopped onion**
   **4 minced garlic cloves**
Stir often for 3 minutes. Add
   **19-oz can tomatoes, drained and chopped**
   **2 tsp ground cumin**
   **½ tsp salt**
   **¼ cup chopped fresh mint or coriander**
Cook, uncovered, stirring and turning chicken
   until tomato mixture is thickened, from 8 to
   10 minutes.
*Makes: 2 to 4 servings*

# Presto Parmigiana Chicken Sauté

Garden-ripe tomatoes mingle with chicken in this quick sauté.

**PREPARATION: 15 MINUTES**
**COOKING: 18 MINUTES**

In a large frying pan over medium, heat
   **1 tsp each butter and olive oil**
Add
   **4 small skinless, boneless chicken breasts
   or 6 thighs**
Sauté until golden, from 3 to 5 minutes per side.
   Push to edge of pan. Add to centre
   **1 finely chopped onion**
   **4 minced garlic cloves**
   **½ tsp salt**
Stir often for 2 minutes. Add
   **4 coarsely chopped seeded large ripe
   tomatoes**
   **¼ tsp each dried basil, leaf oregano and
   pepper**

Cook, uncovered, stirring and turning
   chicken until tomato mixture is thickened,
   from 8 to 10 minutes. Stir into sauce
   **¼ cup freshly grated Parmesan**
Lay on chicken, dividing equally
   **4 slices provolone or mozzarella**
Cover with lid until cheese melts, about
   2 minutes. Terrific on noodles or rice.
   *Makes: 2 servings*

sautés

*Presto Parmigiana Chicken Sauté*

sautés

## Mexican Chicken Sauté

A little hot pepper and chili powder adds Southern heat to this fresh number.

**PREPARATION: 15 MINUTES**
**COOKING: 17 MINUTES**

In a large wide frying pan over medium, heat
  **1 tsp each butter and olive oil**
Add
  **4 small skinless, boneless chicken breasts
    or 6 to 8 thighs**
Sauté until golden, from 3 to 5 minutes per side.
  Push to edge of pan. Add to centre
  **1 finely chopped onion**
  **4 minced garlic cloves**
Stir often for 3 minutes. Add
  **4 coarsely chopped seeded large tomatoes**
  **1 chopped seeded jalapeñô**
    **or ½ tsp hot red pepper flakes**
  **½ tsp chili powder**
  **½ tsp salt**
  **½ cup chopped fresh coriander**
Cook, uncovered, stirring and turning chicken
  until tomato mixture is thickened, from 8 to
  10 minutes.
  *Makes: 2 to 4 servings*

## Chicken & Tomato Curry

Curry doesn't have to mean time-consuming simmering. Here's a recipe, using chicken breasts and tomatoes, that heats up fast.

**PREPARATION: 10 MINUTES**
**COOKING: 16 MINUTES**

In a wide frying pan, heat
  **1 tbsp vegetable oil or butter**
Add
  **1 coarsely chopped large onion**
  **1 minced large garlic clove**
Sprinkle with
  **2 tsp curry powder or 1 tsp each curry
    powder and cumin**
  **⅛ tsp cayenne**

Stir often over medium-low heat for 5 minutes.
  Meanwhile, cut into 1-inch (2.5-cm) cubes
  **4 skinless, boneless chicken breasts**
Increase heat to medium-high. Add chicken and
  stir for 1 minute. Add
  **19-oz can drained tomatoes**
Break tomatoes into bite-size pieces.
  Cover and simmer gently, stirring
  occasionally, for 5 minutes. Add
  **1 cup frozen peas (optional)**
Uncover and simmer, stirring occasionally,
  for 5 minutes.
  *Makes: 4 servings*

## Fast French Chicken Sauté

A little wine or vermouth, a scattering of tarragon and vine-ripened tomatoes add up to *trés magnifique.*

**PREPARATION: 15 MINUTES**
**COOKING: 17 MINUTES**

In a large wide frying pan over medium, heat
  **1 tsp each butter and olive oil**
Add
  **4 small skinless, boneless chicken breasts
    or 6 thighs**
Sauté until golden, from 3 to 5 minutes per side.
  Push to edge of pan. Add to centre
  **1 finely chopped onion**
  **4 minced garlic cloves**
  **½ tsp salt**
Stir often for 3 minutes. Add
  **4 coarsely chopped seeded large ripe
    tomatoes**
  **½ cup white wine or ¼ cup dry vermouth**
  **½ tsp dried tarragon**
  **sprinkle of chopped fresh chervil
    or snipped chives or green onions**
Cook, uncovered, stirring and turning chicken
  until tomato mixture is thickened, from 8 to
  10 minutes.
  *Makes: 2 to 4 servings*

# Fast Curried Chicken

Whip up a complete curried chicken dinner in less than 20 minutes.
Cooked chicken pieces and curry paste make it a cinch.

**PREPARATION: 5 MINUTES**
**COOKING: 13 MINUTES**

In a wide frying pan, heat
    **1 tbsp vegetable oil or butter**
Add
    **1 coarsely chopped onion**
    **1 coarsely chopped sweet pepper**
    **1 coarsely chopped apple**
Sauté over low heat for 3 minutes. Add
    **1 to 2 cups cooked cubed chicken**
    **½ cup chicken broth**
    **1 to 2 tsp curry paste**

Stir until blended. Cover and simmer from
    5 to 10 minutes. Then stir in
    **¼ cup sour cream**
Great served over rice.
    *Makes: 1 to 2 servings*

sautés

*Fast Curried Chicken*

**sautés**

## Classy Italian Sauté

Balsamic vinegar gives an instant elegant edge
to this pretty sauté.

**PREPARATION: 15 MINUTES**
**COOKING: 18 MINUTES**

In a large frying pan over medium, heat
    **1 tsp each butter and olive oil**
Add
    **4 small skinless, boneless breasts**
      **or 6 to 8 thighs**
Sauté until golden, from 3 to 5 minutes per side.
    Push to edge of pan. Add to centre
    **1 finely chopped onion**
    **4 minced garlic cloves**
Stir often for 3 minutes. Add
    **4 coarsely chopped large tomatoes**
    **2 tbsp balsamic vinegar**
    **1 tbsp granulated sugar**
    **½ tsp each dried leaf oregano and basil or**
      **1 tsp chopped fresh oregano and**
      **1 tbsp chopped fresh basil**
    **½ tsp salt**
Cook, uncovered, stirring and turning chicken
    until tomato mixture is thickened, from 8 to
    10 minutes.
    *Makes: 2 to 4 servings*

## Spanish Chicken with Olives

That jar of stuffed olives you have in the pantry or
refrigerator comes in handy in this sauté.

**PREPARATION: 20 MINUTES**
**COOKING: 40 MINUTES**

In a large frying pan over medium, heat
    **1 tbsp olive oil**
Add
    **4 to 6 serving-size, bone-in chicken pieces**
Cook, turning often, until lightly browned on all
    sides, from 8 to 10 minutes. Sprinkle into pan
    **1 coarsely chopped large onion**
    **2 minced garlic cloves**

Stir for about 2 minutes. Add
    **28-oz can whole plum tomatoes,**
      **drained and coarsely chopped**
    **½ cup pimento-stuffed green olives**
    **½ tsp dried leaf thyme**
    **¼ tsp dried leaf oregano**
Cover, then when boiling, reduce heat and
    simmer until chicken feels springy, from
    30 to 40 minutes. Turn often. Great over
    rice or pasta.
    *Makes: 4 to 6 servings*

## Tequila Margarita Chicken

Lively lime blends with a touch of honey and a
splash of tequila in this easy dinner.

**PREPARATION: 15 MINUTES**
**COOKING: 40 MINUTES**

In a frying pan over medium, melt
    **1 tsp butter**
Add, bone-side up
    **4 serving-size pieces bone-in chicken,**
      **(skin removed if you wish)**
Cook, just until lightly browned, about
    5 minutes. Add
    **1 cup chicken broth or bouillon**
    **½ tsp finely grated lime peel**
Cover and simmer, turning chicken at least
    once, until chicken feels springy, from
    30 to 45 minutes.
Remove chicken to a serving platter and cover.
    Increase heat to high. Boil sauce, uncovered,
    stirring often, until reduced to ⅓ cup, about
    5 minutes. Stir in
    **1 tbsp each liquid honey, lime juice and**
      **tequila**
Pour over chicken.
    *Makes: 4 servings*

# Fast Saucy Italian Chicken

Serve this chicken over pasta and you'll have a substantial one-dish dinner that's hard to beat.

**PREPARATION: 10 MINUTES**
COOKING: 35 MINUTES

In a large frying pan over medium,
  bring to a boil
  **2 cups spaghetti sauce**
  **¼ lb (125 g) sliced fresh mushrooms, about**
    **1½ cups**
  **1 diced green pepper**
  **¼ tsp Italian seasoning**
  **¼ tsp hot red pepper flakes**

Then place, meat-side down, in sauce
  **4 skinless, bone-in chicken breasts**
Cover and simmer over low heat, turning several
  times, until chicken feels springy, from 30 to
  40 minutes. Taste and add more Italian
  seasoning if needed.
  *Makes: 4 servings*

**sautés**

## tips
# fast chicken sautés

**Skinless, boneless chicken breasts are the perfect fast food. Here are some easy flavor embellishers for 4 chicken breasts:**

**• Add ½ cup spaghetti sauce and some sliced mushrooms, celery or zucchini to chicken breasts in pan. Stir in ¼ cup red wine if you want. Then simmer, covered, turning often, about 15 minutes. Serve over hot pasta.**

**• Blend ½ cup sour cream with 1 tbsp Dijon and lots of black pepper. Pour over cooked sautéed chicken breasts in a pan and just heat through.**

**• Sauté chicken breasts in butter until golden brown. Sprinkle with cracked black pepper, then squeeze juice of half a lemon over top. Add 4 sliced green onions and simmer, covered, about 12 minutes.**

# soups
## and stews

Chicken soup does have restorative powers (whether it contains matzo balls or not). *Country Italian Chickpea Soup* (see recipe page 110) is brimming with healthy Swiss chard and chickpeas. There's also a Moroccan version with carrots and couscous, an elegant French chicken soup filled with asparagus, a Hot & Sour Oriental Soup and lots more. And then there are stews from paprikash to cacciatore, comfort foods if ever there were.

## Country Italian Chickpea Soup

Combine all the seductive flavors of southern Italy in this substantial yet not overly filling supper soup.

**PREPARATION: 15 MINUTES**
**COOKING: 53 MINUTES**

In a large wide-bottomed saucepan, heat
  **1 tbsp olive oil**
When hot, add
  **1 coarsely chopped large onion**
  **3 minced large garlic cloves**
Stir often over medium heat for 5 minutes.
  To the sautéed onions, add
  **3 to 4 skinless, bone-in chicken breasts or**
    **legs, about 2 lbs (1 kg)**
  **4 cups chicken bouillon or broth**
    **(see recipe page 123)**
  **1 small dried chili, lightly crushed**
    **or ½ tsp hot red pepper flakes**
  **½ tsp dried rosemary**
Bring to a boil. Reduce heat to low, cover and
  simmer for 30 minutes, stirring often. Turn
  chicken. Stir in
  **19-oz can drained chickpeas**
    **or 2 cups drained cooked beans**
  **4 coarsely chopped plum tomatoes**
Continue simmering, covered, until chicken is
  done, another 15 to 20 minutes. Remove
  chicken. Separate from bones. Slice and
  return to the soup. Stir in
  **6 cups shredded Swiss chard**
    **or spinach leaves**
Heat until hot and Swiss chard or spinach is
  done as you like, from 3 to 5 minutes.
Sprinkle each serving with
  **freshly grated Parmesan (optional)**
Soup will keep well, covered, in the refrigerator
  for up to 2 days or freeze.
  *Makes: 8 cups*

## Triple Onion & Chicken Soup

Main-course status and low-fat protein have been added to a terrific onion soup recipe – and all without hours of simmering or using a lot of butter.

**PREPARATION: 15 MINUTES**
**COOKING: 1¼ HOURS**

In a large wide saucepan over medium, heat
  **1 tbsp butter**
When hot, add
  **3 to 4 thickly sliced large red onions,**
    **separated into rounds (about 10 cups)**
  **3 to 4 thickly sliced large white onions,**
    **separated into rounds (about 10 cups)**
Stir often, uncovered, until softened, about
  15 minutes. Increase heat to medium-high
  and, stirring frequently, cook onions until
  golden, from 15 to 20 more minutes. Stir
  almost constantly towards the end of cooking
  time to prevent onions from burning. Add
  **6 cups chicken bouillon or broth**
    **(see recipe page 123)**
  **½ cup white wine or ¼ cup sherry**
  **1½ tsp dried leaf thyme**
  **½ tsp salt**
  **¼ tsp each ground nutmeg and white pepper**
Bring to a boil. Submerge in soup
  **2 to 4 skinless, bone-in chicken breasts**
Reduce heat to low, cover and simmer for
  40 minutes, stirring occasionally. Remove
  chicken, separate from bones, then slice
  chicken into strips and return to soup with
  **4 sliced green onions**
Heat and serve with warm cheese bread.
  Soup will keep well, covered, in the
  refrigerator for up to 2 days or freeze.
  *Makes: 9 cups*

# Moroccan Chicken-Vegetable Soup

This soup gives you a charming hint of the exotic in much less time than it takes to make a tagine – and at a fraction of the cost.

**PREPARATION: 15 MINUTES**
**COOKING: 1 HOUR**

In a large saucepan over high heat, place
  **6 cups chicken bouillon or broth
    (see recipe page 123)
  4 to 6 skinless, bone-in chicken pieces
    or 3 lb (1.5 kg) chicken, cut-up
  2 coarsely chopped large onions,
    preferably red
  6 minced garlic cloves
  2 bay leaves
  1 tsp ground cumin or 2 tsp cumin seeds
  ½ tsp each salt, turmeric and cinnamon**
When boiling, skim off foam, then reduce heat to low. Cover and simmer for 30 minutes, stirring occasionally. Add
  **6 sliced carrots**
Continue cooking, covered, 30 more minutes. Remove chicken and bay leaves. Skim fat from soup surface and discard. Stir in
  **⅓ cup couscous**
Remove from heat and cover. Separate chicken from bones and slice into strips. Return chicken to soup with
  **½ cup sliced green onions**
Soup will keep well, covered, in the refrigerator for up to 2 days or freeze.
  *Makes: 10 cups*

# Chicken Soup with Ginger

Ginger, garlic and fresh basil breathe new life into chicken soup. We guarantee it will still have the same restorative powers.

**PREPARATION: 10 MINUTES**
**COOKING: 47 MINUTES**

In a large pot over medium, combine
  **1 chopped onion
  2 tbsp grated fresh ginger
  2 minced garlic cloves
  ½ cup chicken broth (see recipe page 123)**
Simmer until onion is soft, stirring often, about 5 minutes. Stir in
  **1 tsp Dijon
  5½ cups chicken broth
  1 sprig fresh thyme or ½ tsp dried thyme
  1 bay leaf
  ¼ tsp ground black pepper
  ½ cup barley
  4 skinless, bone-in chicken legs**
Increase heat to high, cover and bring to a boil. Reduce heat and simmer, covered and stirring occasionally, for 25 minutes. Stir in
  **3 thinly sliced carrots**
Continue simmering, covered, 15 more minutes. Stir into soup
  **½ cup each peas and corn kernels,
    fresh or frozen**
Remove chicken. Remove bones and cut chicken into bite-size pieces. Stir into soup with
  **½ cup chopped fresh basil
    or 1 tsp dried basil**
Continue simmering until vegetables are hot, about 2 minutes. Add salt if needed. Soup will keep well, covered, in the refrigerator for up to 2 days or freeze.
  *Makes: 9 cups*

soups and stews

## Hot & Sour Oriental Soup

Ginger and lemon give an Oriental
edge to this very healthy low-fat soup.

**PREPARATION: 20 MINUTES**
**COOKING: 22 MINUTES**

In a large saucepan, bring to a boil
   4 cups chicken bouillon
   4 thick slices fresh ginger
   1 minced large garlic clove
   ½ tsp ground cumin
   ¼ tsp hot red pepper flakes
   2 strips lemon or lime peel, each about
      1x2 inches (2.5x5 cm)
Cover, reduce heat and simmer for 10 minutes.
   Then add
   4 skinless, boneless chicken breasts,
      cut into bite-size pieces
Cover and simmer for 10 more minutes.
   Remove ginger slices and lemon or lime peel.
   Add to broth
   2 cups shredded Chinese or regular cabbage
   ¼ lb (125 g) sliced mushrooms, about 2 cups
   2 sliced green onions
Continue simmering until cabbage is tender-
   crisp, from 2 to 6 minutes. Serve immediately.
   *Makes: 4 servings*

## French Asparagus Soup

Asparagus and spinach provide a refreshing
spring tone to this light soup.

**PREPARATION: 20 MINUTES**
**COOKING: 25 MINUTES**

In a large saucepan, bring to a boil
   4 cups chicken bouillon or broth
      (see recipe page 123)
   ½ cup dry white wine
   1 finely chopped onion
   1 minced small garlic clove
   1 finely diced carrot
   ¼ cup chopped celery leaves (optional)
   pinch of white pepper

Then add
   2 skinless, boneless chicken breasts
Cover, reduce heat and simmer just until chicken
   feels springy, from 10 to 15 minutes. Then
   remove from broth and add
   6 asparagus spears, woody ends removed,
      sliced diagonally into 1-inch (2.5-cm)
      pieces
Continue to simmer, covered, until asparagus
   is almost tender, about 5 minutes. Cut
   chicken into bite-size cubes. Return to
   broth along with
   1 packed cup spinach leaves,
      cut into ½-inch (1-cm) pieces
   2 thinly sliced green onions
Simmer until heated through.
   *Makes: 4 servings*

## Easy Elegant Soup

Asparagus, slivers of mushrooms
and red pepper in a soothing broth add up to
a sophisticated spring starter.

**PREPARATION: 10 MINUTES**
**COOKING: 10 MINUTES**

In a large saucepan, bring to a boil
   2 (10-oz) cans chicken broth,
      preferably low-salt
   2 cups water
   ¼ cup dry sherry
   1 tbsp freshly squeezed lemon juice
   ¼ tsp salt
   4 thin slices fresh ginger
When boiling, stir in
   1 finely chopped small red pepper
   ¼ lb (125 g) thinly sliced fresh mushrooms,
      such as shiitake or button
   2 cups diagonally sliced asparagus
   2 thinly sliced green onions
   1 cup diced cooked chicken
Continue cooking, uncovered, stirring often,
   until asparagus is done as you like, about
   5 minutes. Remove ginger and serve.
   *Makes: 7 cups*

Quickies chicken

# Country French Leek & Chicken Soup

Rich and creamy with big chunks of chicken,
you might well think this hearty soup is laced with heavy cream – yet there's not a drop!

**PREPARATION: 30 MINUTES**
**COOKING: 45 MINUTES**

soups and stews

Slice in half lengthwise
**3 leeks**
Slice off and discard all but 1 inch (2.5 cm) of green part of leek. Gently separate remaining outer leaves and wash under cold running water. Then slice into ½-inch (1-cm) thick pieces. In a large wide saucepan, melt
**1 tbsp butter**
Add leeks and sauté over medium heat until softened, about 10 minutes. Stir in
**4 cups chicken bouillon or broth (see recipe page 123)**
**1 cup white wine or apple juice (optional)**
**4 finely chopped carrots**
**1 tbsp Dijon**
**½ tsp each ground nutmeg, white pepper and salt**

Bring to a boil. Submerge, as much as possible, in boiling soup
**4 to 6 pieces skinless, bone-in chicken**
Cover, reduce heat to low and simmer for 20 minutes. Turn chicken and stir in
**4 diced peeled potatoes**
**3 apples, peeled, cored and cubed**
**2 sliced celery stalks**
Continue simmering, covered, until chicken is cooked, from 15 to 25 minutes. Remove chicken. Separate chicken from bones and slice into bite-size pieces. Stir into hot soup. Add more salt as needed and a refreshing sprinkling of nutmeg just before serving. Soup will keep well, covered, in the refrigerator for up to 3 days.
*Makes: 15 cups*

Country French Leek & Chicken Soup

113

# Garlic & Broccoli Chicken Soup

Chock-full of veggies, chicken and homemade flavor, this satisfying soup will become a family favorite.

**PREPARATION: 25 MINUTES**
**COOKING: 35 MINUTES**

In a large saucepan over medium-high, place
  **6 cups cold water**
  **4 bone-in chicken legs or breasts**
  **1 each sliced onion, celery stalk and
    large carrot**
  **1 whole head garlic,
    separated into unpeeled cloves**
  **1 bay leaf**
  **1 tsp salt**
  **1 sprig fresh thyme or ½ tsp dried leaf thyme**
  **½ tsp hot red pepper flakes or ¼ tsp ground
    black pepper**
Bring to a boil. Skim off foam. Reduce heat, cover and simmer until chicken is cooked, from 30 to 40 minutes. Remove chicken. Strain broth and skim off fat. Remove and discard bay leaf. Remove garlic from vegetables. Squeeze garlic cloves from skins, mash with a fork and stir into broth. Return vegetables to broth. Separate chicken from bones, cut into pieces and return to broth. (At this point, soup can be refrigerated for 2 days or frozen.) Before serving, bring soup to a boil. Stir in
  **1 head broccoli, cut into florets**
Reduce heat to low and simmer, uncovered, until broccoli is tender-crisp and soup is hot, about 3 to 5 minutes.
  *Makes: 8 cups*

VARIATION
*Oriental:* Prepare soup, replacing salt with 2 tbsp soy sauce. Replace broccoli with 2 cups each sliced mushrooms and snow peas and a drained 10-oz can sliced water chestnuts.

# Chunky Chicken Chowder

Definitely a dinner dish. You may want both a fork and a spoon for this substantial soup.

**PREPARATION: 20 MINUTES**
**COOKING: 30 MINUTES**

In a large saucepan over medium, heat
  **1 tbsp butter**
When bubbling, add
  **3 skinless, boneless chicken breasts,
    cut into large, bite-size pieces**
Stir occasionally, until light golden, about 3 minutes. Remove to a bowl. In the pan, melt an additional
  **1 tbsp butter**
Add
  **1 finely chopped onion**
  **1 chopped small red pepper**
  **1 minced garlic clove**
Stir for 3 minutes, then stir in
  **2 cups chicken bouillon or broth
    (see recipe page 123)**
Scrape bottom of pan gently. Add chicken, along with juices, and
  **½ lb (250 g) sliced mushrooms**
  **⅓ cup long-grain rice**
  **⅓ tsp nutmeg**
  **generous pinches of salt and pepper**
Cover, reduce heat and simmer from 15 to 20 minutes, stirring occasionally, until rice is tender and chicken is cooked through. Stir in
  **½ cup whipping, table or sour cream
    (optional)**
Add salt if needed.
  *Makes: 5 cups*

## Skillet Chicken Chili

On the table in 30 minutes,
here's a kid-pleasing supper that adds up to
hearty dining after an active day outdoors.

**PREPARATION: 10 MINUTES**
**COOKING: 20 MINUTES**

In a large frying pan over medium, heat
- 1 tsp vegetable oil

Stir in
- 1 coarsely chopped onion
- 2 minced garlic cloves

Sauté for 4 minutes. Crumble in
- 1 lb (500 g) ground chicken

Sauté until it loses pink color, about 4 minutes.
Stir in
- 19-oz can Mexican-style stewed tomatoes, including juice
- 1 chopped green pepper (optional)
- 1½ tsp chili powder
- 1 tsp ground cumin
- ½ tsp dried leaf oregano
- ¼ tsp salt
- pinch of cinnamon

Bring to a boil. Reduce heat to low, cover and simmer, stirring often, for 10 minutes. Add
- 19-oz can drained kidney, black or Romano beans

Simmer, uncovered, just until hot, about 2 minutes. Terrific with corn bread.
*Makes: 4 servings*

soups
and stews

*Skillet Chicken Chili*

## Poulet Paprikash with Mushrooms

Piquant paprika livens up stove-top
simmered chicken.

**PREPARATION: 10 MINUTES**
**COOKING: 40 MINUTES**

In a large frying pan over medium, melt
   **1 tbsp butter**
When hot, add
   **4 skinless, boneless chicken breasts**
Lightly brown, about 3 minutes per side.
   Remove chicken from pan. Add
   **2 sliced onions**
   **2 minced garlic cloves**
   **½ lb (250 g) sliced mushrooms**
Sprinkle with
   **1 tsp paprika**
   **¼ tsp salt**
   **pinch of cayenne**
Cook, stirring occasionally, until onions soften
   and mushrooms have lost most of their
   moisture, about 7 minutes. Stir in
   **1 sliced green pepper**
   **1 cup chicken bouillon or broth**
   **(see recipe page 123)**
   **2 coarsely chopped unpeeled large tomatoes**
   **or a 19-oz can drained tomatoes**
Break up canned tomatoes, if using. Bring to a
   boil. Return chicken, plus any juices, to pan.
   Reduce heat to low and simmer, uncovered,
   stirring occasionally, for 15 minutes. Remove
   chicken and cover to keep warm. Increase
   heat to medium-high. Boil sauce, uncovered
   and stirring often, until slightly thickened,
   about 8 minutes. Remove from heat and stir
   in sour cream if you like. Serve over chicken
   on a bed of hot noodles or rice.
   *Makes: 4 servings*

## Hungarian Chicken with Red Pepper

This version of chicken paprikash delivers
all the comforting taste of the classic, yet it's
lower in fat. And it's bursting with beta-carotene,
thanks to the peppers and tomatoes.

**PREPARATION: 15 MINUTES**
**COOKING: 15 MINUTES**

In a large heavy-bottomed frying pan over
   medium, place
   **½ coarsely chopped Spanish onion**
      **or 1 coarsely chopped large cooking onion**
   **juice from 19-oz can tomatoes**
   **2 minced garlic cloves**
   **2 tsp paprika, preferably Hungarian**
   **2 tsp granulated sugar**
   **1 tsp caraway seeds**
   **¼ tsp each salt and black pepper**
Cook, uncovered and stirring often, until onion
   softens, about 5 minutes. Stir drained
   tomatoes into softened onion. Break up with
   a fork and continue cooking until bubbly.
   Add to pan
   **4 skinless, boneless chicken breasts,**
      **each cut lengthwise into 5 or 6 long strips**
   **1 julienned sweet red pepper**
Cook, uncovered, stirring often, until chicken
   feels springy, about 5 minutes. Stir in
   **½ cup light sour cream**
Continue cooking just until hot. Do not boil.
   Serve over hot noodles.
   *Makes: 4 servings*

# Chicken Cacciatore for One

If you're home alone with the urge for a chicken dinner, whip up this instant cacciatore.
Chances are you'll have all the ingredients on hand.

**PREPARATION: 10 MINUTES**
**COOKING: 10 MINUTES**

In a frying pan over high heat, pour
   **19-oz can Italian-style stewed tomatoes,**
      **including juice**
   **¼ cup red wine or sherry**
   **¼ tsp cayenne (optional)**
Break tomatoes into bite-size pieces. Boil,
   uncovered, stirring often, at least 3 minutes,
   to thicken. Then add
   **¼ lb (125 g) thickly sliced mushrooms,**
      **about 2 cups**

Continue boiling. Add
   **1 skinless, boneless chicken breast,**
      **sliced into bite-size strips**
Stir often over high until chicken feels springy,
   from 3 to 5 minutes. Toss with noodles, rice
   or couscous.
   *Makes: 1 serving*

**soups
and stews**

*Chicken Cacciatore for One*

chatelaine
food express

**soups and stews**

## Chicken with Wine & Olives

Lusty olives give a distinctive Mediterranean character to this classy tomato-sauced dish.

**PREPARATION: 15 MINUTES**
**COOKING: 1 HOUR**

In a wide frying pan over medium, heat
   1 tbsp olive oil
Add
   4 skinless, bone-in chicken legs
Brown chicken, about 8 minutes per side.
   Remove from pan. Add
   4 minced garlic cloves
   ½ lb (250 g) thickly sliced mushrooms
Sauté until mushrooms release moisture, about
   5 minutes. Add
   28-oz can tomatoes, including juice
   ½ cup dry white wine
   ½ cup black, green or mixed olives
   1 tsp each dried basil and sugar
   ½ tsp dried leaf thyme
Break up tomatoes. Return chicken to pan.
   Bring to a boil, reduce heat to low and
   partially cover. Simmer until chicken feels
   springy, from 35 to 40 minutes. Turn chicken
   partway through. Remove chicken. Boil
   sauce, uncovered, stirring often, over
   medium-high heat until thick, about
   5 minutes. Round out the meal with tiny
   boiled potatoes and steamed spinach.
*Makes: 4 servings*

## Italian Chicken with Mushrooms

You can't miss pleasing every member of the family with this classic, easy-to-make entrée.

**PREPARATION: 15 MINUTES**
**COOKING: 45 MINUTES**

In a large saucepan over medium heat, combine
   2 (19-oz) cans Italian-style stewed tomatoes,
      including juice
   ½ lb (250 g) thickly sliced mushrooms,
      about 3 cups
   ¼ cup dry red wine
Bring to a boil, stirring often. Place bone-side up
   in sauce
   4 skinless, bone-in chicken breasts or legs
Cover, reduce heat and simmer for 30 minutes.
   Turn chicken and stir in
   ½ lb (250 g) thickly sliced mushrooms,
      about 3 cups
   1 to 2 chopped green peppers
Continue simmering, uncovered, stirring
   occasionally, until chicken is springy, from
   10 to 20 minutes. Remove chicken and
   vegetables. If sauce is not as thick as you like,
   increase heat and boil, uncovered, stirring
   often. Then pour over chicken and vegetables.
   Serve over hot noodles, pasta or rice.
*Makes: 4 servings*

# Creamy Chicken Stew Dijonnaise

This is really a racy rendition of a mom-style chicken stew. If you're not a brussels sprout lover, use broccoli instead.

**PREPARATION: 20 MINUTES**
**COOKING: 20 MINUTES**

Trim away tough stem ends and cut an "X" into base of
**4 cups brussels sprouts**
Cook in salted boiling water until tender, from 8 to 10 minutes. Meanwhile, in a large saucepan over medium-high, heat
**3 tbsp olive oil**
Add
**8 skinless, boneless chicken breasts, cut into 1½-inch (4-cm) cubes**
**½ lb (250 g) peeled baby carrots**
Stir often until it is lightly browned, from 3 to 4 minutes.

Add
**10-oz can cream of chicken soup**
**½ cup dry white wine**
**2 tbsp Dijon**
**2 tsp dried tarragon**
**½ tsp freshly ground black pepper**
Stir until well blended. Bring mixture to a boil over medium heat. Then cover, reduce heat to low and simmer gently, stirring occasionally, until chicken is cooked through, about 8 minutes. Stir in well-drained sprouts and just heat through.
*Makes: 6 servings*

soups and stews

*Creamy Chicken Stew Dijonnaise*

## Vin Blanc Coq au Vin

*Use Chardonnay in the recipe, then sip the remainder, well chilled, with dinner.*

**PREPARATION: 25 MINUTES**
COOKING: 1¼ HOURS

In a wide saucepan over medium, heat
**1 tbsp vegetable oil**
Add to hot oil, about half of
**4-lb (2-kg) chicken, cut into 10 pieces (skin removed if you wish)**
When chicken is golden on both sides, about 5 minutes per side, transfer to a bowl. Repeat with remaining chicken. Then add to pan
**1 sliced onion**
**2 sliced carrots**
**½ lb (250 g) sliced shiitake, button or oyster mushrooms**
**2 minced garlic cloves**
Stir often, for 3 minutes or until onion begins to soften. Set vegetables aside with chicken. Add to pan
**1 tbsp butter**
**3 tbsp flour**
Stir constantly, scraping pan bottom gently, until flour is golden, about 2 minutes. Then gradually whisk in
**2 cups good-quality dry white wine**
**1 tsp dried leaf thyme**
**½ tsp freshly ground black pepper**
**¼ tsp salt**
**1 bay leaf**
Bring to a boil, stirring constantly. Add chicken and vegetables. Reduce heat and simmer gently, covered, stirring occasionally, until chicken is cooked through, about 1 hour. Serve sprinkled with
**3 thinly sliced green onions**
Stew will keep well, covered, in the refrigerator for at least 2 days or freeze.
*Makes: 5 to 6 servings*

## Instant Coq au Vin

*A fast herbed mushroom sauce with French leanings adds class to boneless breasts.*

**PREPARATION: 10 MINUTES**
COOKING: 12 MINUTES

In a large wide frying pan over medium-high, heat
**3 tbsp butter**
Add
**4 skinless, boneless chicken breasts**
Brown on one side, about 2 minutes, then turn and add to pan
**¼ lb (125 g) sliced mushrooms**
**1 minced large garlic clove**
Continue cooking over medium-high heat for 2 more minutes, stirring mushrooms occasionally. Then add
**1 cup white wine**
**½ tsp dried leaf thyme**
**½ tsp granulated sugar**
Continue cooking over medium-high heat until wine is gently boiling, about 2 minutes. Turn chicken and stir mushrooms. Continue cooking, uncovered, until chicken feels springy, from 3 to 5 more minutes. Remove chicken to a platter and place mushrooms on top of chicken. Cover to keep warm. Increase heat to high and stir into wine mixture in pan
**2 sliced green onions**
Stir occasionally until wine is reduced to about ½ cup. Taste and add salt and pepper as needed. Pour wine over chicken and mushrooms. Serve over rice with green peas.
*Makes: 4 servings*

# Light Chicken Goulash

While goulash may conjure visions of gooey flour stew, not so with this streamlined quick-cooking version.

**PREPARATION: 15 MINUTES**
**COOKING: 22 MINUTES**

In a large wide frying pan over medium, heat
   **1 tbsp butter**
When hot, add
   **4 skinless, boneless chicken breasts**
Cook until golden, from 3 to 5 minutes per side.
   Remove from pan. Add to pan
   **1 large onion, sliced into rounds**
   **1 minced garlic clove**
Sauté until softened, 5 minutes. Sprinkle with
   **2 tbsp paprika**
   **2 tbsp all-purpose flour**
   **¾ tsp salt**
   **¼ tsp each granulated sugar and cayenne**

Stir until absorbed, then stir in
   **1 cup chicken bouillon or broth**
Bring to a boil, stirring often until thickened and
   bubbly. Then cut chicken into 1-inch
   (2.5-cm) strips and add with
   **6 plum or 4 regular tomatoes,**
      **seeded and chopped**
   **1 large green pepper,**
      **cut into bite-size pieces (optional)**
Cover and simmer, stirring often, until chicken
   is done, 6 to 10 minutes. Stir in
   **¼ to ½ cup light sour cream (optional)**
Serve over noodles, rice or herbed pasta.
   *Makes: 4 servings*

**soups
and stews**

*Light Chicken Goulash*

soups and stews

## Lemon Chicken Tagine

This intriguing Moroccan-style update on
chicken stew needs no browning or flour.

**PREPARATION: 15 MINUTES**
**COOKING: 55 MINUTES**

In a large wide-bottomed saucepan over medium,
heat
  **1 tbsp olive oil**
Add and sauté for 2 minutes
  **1 Spanish onion or 2 cooking onions, sliced**
  **2 minced garlic cloves**
Then add
  **1 whole chicken, quartered, or 4 chicken**
  **breasts or legs (skin removed if you wish)**
Sprinkle with
  **1 tsp each ground cumin, ginger and paprika**
  **¼ tsp each hot red pepper flakes and freshly**
  **ground black pepper**
Turn chicken often until evenly coated with
  spices, about 3 minutes. Do not brown. Stir in
  **finely grated peel of 1 lemon, about 1 tsp**
  **2 cups chicken bouillon or broth**
  **(see recipe page 123)**
  **2 sliced carrots**
  **½ cup cracked or stuffed green olives**
Bring to a boil. Then cover and reduce heat to
  low. Simmer for 20 minutes. Turn chicken
  and continue simmering until chicken feels
  springy, from 20 to 30 more minutes. Remove
  chicken pieces. Increase heat to medium-high
  and boil gently, uncovered, stirring often,
  until sauce has reduced slightly, from 6 to
  10 minutes. Return chicken to sauce. Stir in
  **½ cup chopped fresh coriander or parsley**
Serve with crusty bread for dipping into sauce or
  spoon over hot couscous. Tagine will keep
  well, covered, in the refrigerator for up to
  3 days or freeze.
*Makes: 4 servings*

## Mediterranean Chicken

An olive lover's dream, this saucy dinner
is tremendous over pasta.

**PREPARATION: 15 MINUTES**
**COOKING: 55 MINUTES**

Cut into 10 pieces
  **4-lb (2-kg) chicken, skin removed**
Sprinkle with
  **salt and freshly ground black pepper**
In a large wide saucepan over medium, heat
  **1 tbsp olive oil**
In 2 batches, cook chicken, uncovered, until
  golden, about 5 minutes per side. Remove
  chicken and set aside. Drain all but
  1 tablespoon fat from pan. Add
  **1 chopped onion**
  **4 minced garlic cloves**
Sauté for about 3 minutes. Add
  **28-oz can diced tomatoes, including juice**
  **1 cup chicken bouillon or broth**
  **(see recipe page 123)**
  **½ cup dry white wine**
  **½ cup each brine-cured black olives and**
  **pimento-stuffed green olives**
  **2 tsp dried leaf basil**
  **1 tsp each dried thyme and oregano**
Return chicken and any juices to pan. When
  boiling, reduce heat, cover and simmer,
  stirring often until chicken is cooked,
  from 30 to 40 minutes. Add
  **2 zucchini, thinly sliced on the diagonal**
Stew will keep well, covered, in the refrigerator
  for up to 2 days or freeze.
*Makes: 4 servings*

# Best Chicken Broth

Chicken broth may need a few hours on the stove, but nothing beats homemade broth for flavor.
Keep this broth handy in the refrigerator or the freezer.

**PREPARATION: 10 MINUTES**

**COOKING: 2 HOURS**

In a large saucepan, place
**2 lbs (1 kg) chicken carcasses or bones**
Cover with
**12 cups water**
Add
**2 coarsely chopped onions**
**2 sliced carrots**
**a handful of celery leaves**
**1 bay leaf**
**1 tsp salt**

Bring to a boil, then reduce heat and simmer, covered, from 2 to 3 hours. Stir occasionally and skim the surface. Strain the stock through a sieve, discarding bones and vegetables. Refrigerate. When cold, skim the layer of fat from the top and discard. Store broth, covered, in the refrigerator for several days or in the freezer for months.
*Makes: 12 cups*

**soups
and stews**

## tips
## soup kitchen

• The quality of a broth or stock is the secret to a great soup. In most cases, it is this quality that intensifies the soup's background flavor. Good homemade chicken broth is usually the best (see recipe above). However, if you don't have time to make your own broth, many specialty grocery stores sell containers of homemade broth. Condensed canned chicken broth is sold in the soup section of most supermarkets as well as sodium-reduced chicken broth. The manufacturers intend the broth to be used with an equal amount of water, but often our recipes call for the condensed soup without added water because liquid is coming from other sources in the recipe such as vegetables.

• The many-flavored cans of stewed tomatoes work well as a soup base and deliver a lot more flavor for the price in the winter than fresh tomatoes. Canned cocktail juice also makes a great base.

• When a soup calls for fresh herbs, it's always a good idea to add an extra light sprinkling just before serving for a fresh taste. A little finely minced garlic or grated orange or lemon peel also adds a refreshing quality if sprinkled over the soup just before serving.

# stir-fries

Fresh flavors soar in stir-fries and each bite delivers a multiplicity of textures. In *Fast Oriental Chicken* (see recipe page 126), moist chicken strips and silky pasta are coated with a garlicky ginger-and-sesame infused Asian sauce.

## Fast Oriental Chicken

Moist chicken and silky pasta are richly coated with a garlic, ginger and sesame Oriental sauce.

**PREPARATION: 10 MINUTES**
**COOKING: 10 MINUTES**

In a large pot of boiling salted water, cook until al dente, about 8 minutes
  **½ (1-lb/450-g) pkg spaghetti or linguine**
Meanwhile, stir together in a medium-size dish until dissolved
  **2 tbsp soy sauce**
  **½ tsp sesame oil**
  **1 tbsp cornstarch**
Add and stir until coated
  **3 skinless, boneless chicken breasts, sliced into thin strips**
Then heat in a large heavy-bottomed frying pan or wok over medium heat
  **1 tbsp peanut or vegetable oil**
Add
  **2 tsp freshly grated ginger or bottled minced ginger**
  **1 minced large garlic clove or ½ tsp bottled minced garlic**
Stir for 1 minute, then add coated chicken and stir often until chicken feels springy, from 4 to 6 minutes. Drain pasta and add to frying pan. Sprinkle with
  **1 tbsp soy sauce**
  **½ tsp sesame oil**
  **3 thinly sliced green onions**
Toss until evenly mixed.
  *Makes: 4 to 6 servings*

## Chicken, Broccoli & Sweet Pepper Stir-Fry

Fresh flavors soar in this colorful dinner that's ready in less than 20 minutes.

**PREPARATION: 10 MINUTES**
**COOKING: 9 MINUTES**

In a small bowl, stir together
  **1 cup chicken broth**
  **3 tbsp soy sauce**
  **1½ tsp freshly grated ginger or bottled minced ginger**
  **1 minced large garlic clove or ½ tsp bottled minced garlic**
  **¼ tsp freshly ground black pepper or cayenne**
In another bowl, stir until dissolved
  **1½ tbsp cornstarch**
  **1 tbsp water**
In a large frying pan over medium-high, heat
  **2 tbsp peanut oil**
When very hot, add
  **3 skinless, boneless chicken breasts, cut into bite-size pieces**
Stir-fry until golden, about 4 minutes. Immediately add broth mixture and
  **1 head broccoli, cut into florets**
  **1 sliced sweet pepper**
Stir often for 2 minutes. While stirring constantly, drizzle in cornstarch mixture. Stir constantly until sauce is thickened, about 3 to 4 minutes. Serve over rice.
  *Makes: 4 servings*

# Teriyaki Ground Chicken Stir-Fry

Less than a pound of inexpensive ground chicken joins lots of fresh veggies in this swift stir-fry that has bits of moist chicken in every colorful bite.

**PREPARATION: 15 MINUTES**
**COOKING: 18 MINUTES**

Whisk together until cornstarch is dissolved
  **10-oz can undiluted chicken broth,
    preferably salt-reduced**
  **2 tbsp cornstarch**
  **2 tbsp teriyaki sauce**
  **1 tbsp brown sugar**
  **1 tbsp freshly grated ginger
    or ½ tsp ground ginger**
  **¼ tsp cayenne**
In a large heavy-bottomed nonstick frying pan or wok over medium, heat
  **1 tbsp olive oil**
When hot, crumble in
  **¾ lb (375 g) ground chicken or turkey**
Stirring often, keep separating chicken with a fork until it just loses its pink color, from 3 to 4 minutes.

Remove chicken to a plate, then add to pan
  **6 cups mixed fresh vegetables, such as broccoli florets, snow peas, red pepper strips, thinly sliced carrots and celery, or 2 (1-lb/500-g) pkgs frozen stir-fry vegetables**
Stirring frequently, sauté until they just start to soften, about 3 minutes. Return chicken to pan and add
  **4 sliced green onions**
Stir sauce, then pour into pan. Increase heat to medium-high. Stir-fry until sauce thickens and vegetables are done as you like, from 3 to 6 minutes. (If using fresh vegetables, cover pan between stirrings to steam.) For extra zing, squeeze fresh lemon or lime juice over top. Serve on a bed of Oriental noodles, angel-hair pasta or brown rice to soak up all the flavorful sauce.

*Makes: 3 to 4 servings, about 7 cups*

stir-fries

Teriyaki Ground Chicken Stir-Fry

stir-fries

## New Pineapple Chicken

Here's a sophisticated new version of pineapple chicken with undertones of caramel and ginger. Besides its winning flavor, it's fast, low in fat and high in protein.

**PREPARATION: 10 MINUTES**
**COOKING: 12 MINUTES**

Into a bowl, drain juice from
    **19-oz can pineapple chunks**
Stir in until dissolved
    **2 tbsp cornstarch**
In a large heavy-bottomed frying pan or wok over medium-high, heat
    **1 tbsp peanut or vegetable oil**
When hot, add
    **4 skinless, boneless chicken breasts, sliced into thin strips**
Stir frequently, until golden, about 3 minutes. Remove chicken and set aside. Add to pan
    **¼ cup white vinegar**
    **3 tbsp granulated sugar**
Stir until sugar dissolves and liquid turns golden, about 2½ minutes. Add
    **¾ cup chicken broth or bouillon**
Stir in pineapple juice mixture, drained pineapple and
    **1 tbsp grated fresh ginger**
    **½ tsp hot red pepper flakes (optional)**
Stir often, until liquid loses its cloudy appearance, about 3 minutes. Add chicken, plus any juice, and
    **4 sliced green onions**
Stir until hot, from 3 to 5 minutes. Add salt and pepper to taste. Serve over noodles or rice.
*Makes: 4 servings*

## Italian Chicken Stir-Fry

Tomatoes, instead of soy sauce, give refreshing moisture to this easy skillet dinner.

**PREPARATION: 15 MINUTES**
**COOKING: 8 MINUTES**

In a large heavy-bottomed saucepan or wok, heat
    **2 tbsp olive or vegetable oil**
When hot, add
    **2 minced garlic cloves**
    **4 skinless, boneless chicken breasts, sliced into thin strips**
Stir-fry over medium-high until chicken is no longer pink, about 2 minutes. Add
    **¼ lb (125 g) green beans, cut in half, or 2 cups frozen green beans**
    **1 coarsely chopped red pepper**
    **1 sliced zucchini**
Continue to stir-fry just until vegetables are tender-crisp, from 2 to 4 minutes. Stir in
    **2 large tomatoes, cut into wedges**
    **2 green onions, cut into 1-inch (2.5-cm) pieces**
    **1 tbsp capers (optional)**
Sprinkle with
    **½ tsp Italian seasoning or dried basil**
    **freshly ground black pepper**
    **2 tbsp freshly squeezed lemon juice**
Stir-fry until piping hot, from 2 to 4 more minutes. Serve over noodles or rice.
*Makes: 4 servings*

# Simply a Stir-Fry

For a home-cooked dinner in minutes, raid your vegetable drawer for whatever needs to be used up. Then stir together a sauce straight from the pantry.

**PREPARATION: 15 MINUTES**
**COOKING: 8 MINUTES**

Stir together until cornstarch is dissolved
- ⅓ **cup water**
- ¼ **cup soy or teriyaki sauce**
- **1 tbsp cornstarch**
- **1 tbsp maple syrup or sugar**
- **1 tsp Italian seasoning**
- ¼ **tsp black or cayenne pepper**

In a large frying pan over medium-high, heat
- **1 tbsp vegetable oil**

Add
- **2 minced garlic cloves**

- **6 to 8 cups mixed fresh vegetables, such as broccoli florets, thinly sliced zucchini, peppers, onions and celery, or 2 (1-lb/500-g) pkgs frozen stir-fry vegetables.**

Stir-fry for 2 minutes. Stir sauce and add to pan. Stir constantly until vegetables are hot but still crisp, from 4 to 8 minutes. Stir in
- **3 cups cooked thin strips of chicken**

Heat through and serve over hot rice or toss with pasta.

*Makes: 4 servings*

stir-fries

*Simply a Stir-Fry*

chatelaine
food express

*stir-fries*

## Orange-Glazed Stir-Fry

Please your youngsters with this stir-fry – orange juice gives it a familiar taste and it's not too hot.

**PREPARATION: 10 MINUTES**
**COOKING: 8 MINUTES**

In a bowl, whisk together
  ½ cup chicken bouillon
  1 tbsp each orange juice concentrate
    and soy sauce
  2 tsp cornstarch
  freshly ground black pepper
In a large heavy-bottomed frying pan or wok,
  heat
  1 to 2 tbsp vegetable oil
When hot, add
  4 skinless, boneless chicken breasts,
    sliced into thin strips
Stir-fry over medium-high heat for 2 minutes.
  Immediately add
  1 minced garlic clove
  3 sliced green onions
  4 thinly sliced carrots
Add bouillon mixture. Stir until sauce is
  thickened and vegetables and chicken are
  cooked, from 4 to 6 minutes. Taste and add
  salt if needed.
  *Makes: 4 servings*

## Fast 'n' Healthy Stir-Fry

This will become a "count-on" dinner, since kitchen staples create a flavorful sauce for whatever's stashed in your fridge.

**PREPARATION: 15 MINUTES**
**COOKING: 8 MINUTES**

Stir together until cornstarch is dissolved
  ½ cup water
  ¼ cup soy sauce
  1 tbsp cornstarch
  1 tbsp brown sugar or honey
  ¾ tsp ground ginger
  ½ tsp chili powder
  ¼ tsp each garlic powder and black pepper
In a large heavy-bottomed frying pan or wok
  over medium-high, heat
  2 tbsp vegetable or peanut oil
Add
  4 skinless, boneless chicken breasts, sliced
    into thin strips
Stir-fry until golden, about 3 minutes. Stir sauce
  and add to wok along with
  8 cups mixed fresh vegetables, such as
    broccoli florets, snow peas, red pepper
    strips and thinly sliced carrots and celery,
    or 2 (1-lb/500-g) pkgs frozen stir-fry
    vegetables
Stir-fry until vegetables are hot but still crisp,
  from 5 to 8 minutes. If using fresh vegetables,
  cover pan between stirrings to steam. Don't
  cover frozen vegetables. Great over rice.
  *Makes: 6 servings*

# Peppery Liver Stir-Fry

Chicken livers are perfect for stir-frying. Here they mingle with mushrooms
and peppers for a delightful after-work meal.

**PREPARATION: 10 MINUTES**
**COOKING: 9 MINUTES**

In a large heavy-bottomed frying pan or wok
   over medium, heat
   **2 tbsp vegetable oil**
Add
   **1 lb (500 g) chicken livers, halved**
Gently stir over medium heat for 2 minutes.
   Remove livers from the pan and cover to keep
   warm. Add to pan
   **¼ lb (125 g) sliced mushrooms**
Slice into ¼-inch (0.5-cm) strips and add to
   the pan
   **2 onions**

**1 red pepper**
**1 green pepper**
Stir-fry over medium-high heat for 4 minutes.
   Return livers to the pan. Add
   **⅓ cup dry red wine**
   **1 tsp dried rosemary**
Sprinkle with
   **pinches of salt and freshly ground black
   pepper**
Stir gently and often, from 3 to 4 minutes.
   Serve over a bed of rice.
   *Makes: 4 servings*

**stir-fries**

## tips
## wok talk

The keys to any successful stir-frying are organization and pre-prep.

• Assemble and prepare all ingredients before you begin to cook. Since cooking time is short, there is no time to complete any preparation once cooking has started.

• The intensity of the heat is very important. An easily controlled high heat is essential so that food will begin to cook as soon as it is added to the oil.

• Cooking utensils needed to stir-fry include a large heavy-bottomed frying pan or wok and a wooden spoon or Chinese metal spatula. Since all ingredients have to be tossed rapidly, a wok has distinct advantages, but most dishes can be made in a deep wide frying pan.

• For even cooking, poultry, meat, fish and vegetables should be cut into pieces of equal size.

• If using a wok, a 14-inch (35-cm) diameter carbon-steel type is a good choice. There are also excellent electric woks available. Some woks have a flat bottom, making them ideal for electric burners — contact between the wok and the burner provides a more even distribution of heat. The sides of the pan also become hot, thereby cooking food as it is tossed around the edges of the pan.

• To prevent food from sticking, a wok should be cleaned and seasoned with oil before using to seal grooves that exist in the carbon steel. The more a wok is used, the more seasoned it becomes.

# wraps

Wraps denote relaxed dining. They're perfect for creamy chicken in a baked party casserole as in our ***Baked Chicken Wraps*** (see recipe page 134) or filled with a tropical salad mixture, seasoned leftover roasted chicken or a paprikash sour cream. Get ready to roll.

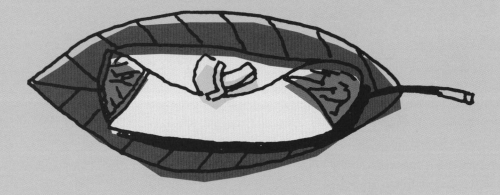

wraps

## Baked Chicken Wraps

These creamy wraps – a thoroughly modern way to use leftover chicken or roast – are a big hit with hungry teenagers.

**PREPARATION: 20 MINUTES**
**BAKING: 30 MINUTES**

Preheat oven to 350°F (180°C). In the bottom of a 9x13-inch (3-L) baking dish, spread
**½ (19-oz) can flavored chunky tomatoes, such as spicy red pepper, roasted garlic and basil or sun-dried tomatoes**

Whisk together
**10-oz can undiluted cream of mushroom or chicken soup**
**½ cup light or regular sour cream**
**1 tsp hot pepper sauce**

It will not be completely smooth. Stir in
**3 cups cooked chicken or turkey**
**½ cup grated old cheddar or Monterey Jack cheese**
**2 thinly sliced green onions**

Lay flat on cutting board or counter
**8 flour tortillas**

Divide chicken mixture evenly among tortillas, mounding in a row slightly off-centre. Roll into a cigar shape around filling and place seam-side down in baking dish. Spoon remaining tomatoes, including juice, over top, then sprinkle with
**1 cup grated old cheddar or Monterey Jack cheese**

Bake, uncovered, until cheese is golden, from 30 to 35 minutes. Great with a mixed green salad.

*Makes: 8 wraps, for 3 to 4 servings*

## Chicken Enchiladas

Roll this creamy chicken-and-salsa mixture into tortillas for a comfort food with a little zing.

**PREPARATION: 20 MINUTES**
**COOKING: 8 MINUTES**
**BAKING: 30 MINUTES**

Preheat oven to 350°F (180°C). In a medium-size frying pan over medium, heat
**1 tsp vegetable oil**

When hot, add
**1 coarsely chopped onion**
**1 minced garlic clove**
**½ tsp each chili powder and ground cumin**

Stir occasionally until onion has softened, about 5 minutes. Add
**4-oz (125-g) pkg light or regular cream cheese**

Break up cheese until melted. Blend in
**½ cup salsa**

Remove from heat and stir in
**3 cups cooked chicken or turkey strips**
**½ cup grated old cheddar or Monterey Jack cheese**
**¼ cup pitted sliced black olives**

Over bottom of a 9x13-inch (3-L) baking dish, spread
**½ (19-oz) can Mexican-style stewed tomatoes, including juice**

Lay flat on cutting board or counter
**8 flour tortillas**

Divide chicken mixture evenly among tortillas, mounding in a row slightly off-centre. Roll into a cigar shape around filling and place seam-side down on sauce in baking dish. Spoon remaining tomatoes over top and sprinkle with
**1 cup grated old cheddar or Monterey Jack cheese**

Bake, uncovered, until cheese is golden, from 30 to 35 minutes. Serve with a green salad.

*Makes: 8 enchiladas, for 3 to 4 servings*

## Fun Fajitas

If you like fajitas fiery, top with lots of hot salsa,
a smattering of chopped avocado and a drizzle of
sour cream. Then wrap and eat.

**PREPARATION: 15 MINUTES**
**COOKING: 10 MINUTES**

In a large frying pan over medium, heat
   1 tbsp vegetable or olive oil
When hot, add
   1 sliced onion
   2 minced garlic cloves
   1 sliced sweet pepper
   4 skinless, boneless chicken breasts,
      sliced into thin strips
   1½ tsp each chili powder and cumin
   ¼ tsp each leaf oregano, salt and pepper
Stir often, until chicken is cooked through, from
   8 to 10 minutes. Spoon mixture over
   8 warm flour tortillas or pitas
Dividing evenly, top with
   ½ to ¾ cup salsa
   1 chopped avocado
   ¾ cup sour cream
*Makes: 8 fajitas, for 3 to 4 servings*

## Smoked Chicken Rolls

Dinner in a hurry can be as simple as rolling
up a tortilla with healthy ingredients.

**PREPARATION: 10 MINUTES**

Slice into bite-size strips
   8 oz (250 g) sliced smoked chicken
Stir together
   ½ cup light sour cream
   grated peel of 1 lime
   ¼ tsp hot pepper sauce
Lay flat
   6 tortillas
Divide chicken strips evenly among tortillas,
   mounding in a row slightly off-centre.

Dividing evenly, top with
   3 grated carrots
   1 sliced avocado
Dab with sour cream mixture. Scatter with
   chopped fresh coriander or thinly sliced
      green onions
Top with a little lettuce if you wish. Roll into a
   cigar shape and slice in half diagonally.
   *Makes: 6 tortilla rolls, for 2 to 3 servings*

## Roasted-Chicken Fajitas

To easily satisfy a crowd with flavor-your-own
fajitas, use leftovers from a roast chicken or buy a
barbecued chicken.

**PREPARATION: 15 MINUTES**
**COOKING: 10 MINUTES**

In a large frying pan over medium, heat
   1 tbsp vegetable or olive oil
Add
   2 onions, sliced into thin strips
   2 sweet red peppers, sliced into thin strips
   2 minced garlic cloves
Sprinkle with
   3 tsp chili powder
   1 tsp each cumin and dried leaf oregano
   ½ tsp freshly ground black pepper
   ¼ tsp salt
Stir frequently until soft, about 5 minutes,
   adding more oil if needed. Then add
   4 to 6 cups roasted chicken strips
Stir until hot. Spoon onto a large platter. Set out
   in separate bowls
   3 coarsely chopped tomatoes
   1 chopped avocado
   fresh coriander sprigs
   salsa
   sour cream
   16 warm tortillas
Have guests spoon chicken mixture onto tortillas,
   add toppings they like and then roll.
   *Makes: 16 fajitas, for 6 to 8 servings*

wraps

135

## Avocado & Chicken Salad Wraps

The avocado raises these wraps to a terrific summer muncher.

**PREPARATION: 15 MINUTES**
**COOKING: 12 MINUTES**

Flatten slightly, by pounding with your fist
  **4 skinless, boneless chicken breasts**
In a large nonstick frying pan over medium, heat
  **2 tsp olive oil**
Sauté chicken until it feels springy, from 6 to 8 minutes per side. When chicken is cooked, slice into strips. Toss with
  **2 chopped seeded tomatoes**
  **2 sliced green onions**
  **¼ cup Dijonnaise**
    **or 2 tbsp each Dijon and mayonnaise**
  **¼ tsp salt**
  **pinch of cayenne (optional)**
Gently stir in
  **1 cubed avocado**
Roll or stuff mixture into
  **6 tortillas or 4 pitas, halved**
Sprinkle with
  **chopped fresh coriander**
*Makes: 6 wraps or 8 halves, for 3 to 4 servings*

## Cheater Chicken Paprikash Wraps

Here's a hearty yet fun homemade dinner that's ready in 20 minutes.

**PREPARATION: 5 MINUTES**
**COOKING: 18 MINUTES**

In a large frying pan over medium-high, place
  **¾ cup rosé or white wine**
  **1 thinly sliced large onion**
  **1 tsp paprika**
Boil gently, uncovered and stirring often, until onion has softened, about 5 minutes. Stir in
  **4 skinless, boneless chicken breasts, sliced into strips**

Reduce heat to medium-low and stir often, uncovered, until chicken is cooked, about 10 minutes. Remove chicken to a warm plate and cover. Increase heat to medium-high and boil down sauce, uncovered and stirring often, until about ½ cup remains, from 3 to 5 minutes. Whisk in
  **⅓ cup regular sour cream**
Pour over chicken. Spoon onto
  **4 warm flour tortillas or pitas, halved**
*Makes: 4 wraps or 8 halves, for 3 to 4 servings*

## Salsa-Spiked Rolls

Keep ground chicken and tortillas in the freezer for whenever you need a casual quick-fix dinner.

**PREPARATION: 10 MINUTES**
**COOKING: 10 MINUTES**

In a large frying pan over medium, heat
  **1 tbsp vegetable oil**
When hot, add
  **1 lb (500 g) ground chicken**
  **1 chopped onion**
  **2 chopped celery stalks**
  **1 chopped green pepper**
  **1 tsp cumin**
  **½ tsp each chili powder and salt**
Stir often, keeping chicken separated, until onion is soft, from 8 to 12 minutes. Stir in
  **1 cup salsa**
  **¼ tsp hot pepper sauce**
Stir until hot. Lay flat on cutting board or counter
  **6 flour tortillas**
Lightly spread with
  **sour cream**
Divide chicken mixture evenly among tortillas, mounding in a row slightly off-centre. Roll into a cigar shape around filling.
*Makes: 6 rolls, for 3 servings*

# Tropical Chicken Sandwich with Mango Mayonnaise

Ripe mango and a sprinkling of toasted coconut give a
Caribbean twist to these moist pocket sandwiches.

**PREPARATION: 10 MINUTES**

Peel, then slice pulp from
   **1 small ripe mango**
Thinly slice half the pulp and set aside. Mash the
   remainder with a fork. You should have about
   ½ cup. Stir into
   **¼ cup light mayonnaise**
Slice off top edge of
   **6 pitas**
Evenly stuff into pitas
   **1 lb (500 g) sliced roasted chicken or turkey**
Drizzle chicken with a little mango mayonnaise.
   Top with sliced mango and
   **2 cups shredded iceberg lettuce**

Add more mango mayonnaise and sprinkle with
   **½ cup chopped toasted cashews or almonds**
If making ahead, the ingredients can be prepared
   and refrigerated before making sandwiches.
For a wonderful open-face party sandwich,
   spread mango mayonnaise over thick slices of
   crusty white bread or shaped cutouts. Top
   with shredded lettuce, thin slices of chicken
   and a dollop of mango mayonnaise. Decorate
   with mango slices and a sprinkling of
   chopped nuts and toasted coconut.
*Makes: 6 sandwiches*

wraps

*Tropical Chicken Sandwich with Mango Mayonnaise*

# Tips for delicious, healthy chicken

## Skinning Chicken Breasts

- Removing the skin from chicken breasts, either before or after cooking, reduces fat and calories significantly (142 calories and 3 grams of fat per half without skin, compared with 193 calories and 8 grams of fat with skin).

- Leaving skin on for roasting prevents drying of the delicate chicken. Just don't eat it.

- To remove skin before cooking, place chicken breasts, skin-side up, on a clean surface. Grasp skin with a piece of paper towel and pull skin away. Cut off any strips of solid white fat. Discard the skin and fat.

## Boneless Chicken Thighs

- For a fraction of the cost of boneless breasts, you can easily prepare boneless chicken thighs. Place thighs, skin-side down, on a cutting board. With a sharp knife, cut down the middle, lengthwise, to the single straight bone. Scrape flesh away from bone, pull out bone and flatten thigh. Cut away any yellow fat and remove skin if you wish.

- Use boneless thighs just as you would boneless breasts — they cook almost as fast and have more flavor. Count on two thighs for each breast called for in recipe. Freeze the bones for chicken stock.

- Skinless chicken thighs have approximately the same nutrients as skinless chicken breasts and no more fat. A fried chicken wing, however, has 7 grams of fat.

## Boning Chicken Breasts

1. **Holding the breast half in both hands, bend and break the large bone in the chicken breast.**

2. **Run your thumb between the meat and the large bone, removing the strip of cartilage.**

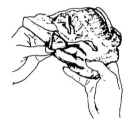

3. **Using both thumbs, loosen the meat from around the rib cage.**

4. **Pull or scrape the breast meat away from the bones. If a small piece of bone remains, pull it out or cut it out with a knife.**

## Tips for Great-Tasting Chicken

- Keep marinating time short or you'll over-power chicken's delicate taste. Stick to two hours or less for a highly seasoned marinade or up to four hours for a mild one.

- Rub seasonings into chicken — including salt and pepper. If you sprinkle seasonings, the flavors will end up in the pan juices.

- Don't overcrowd chicken pieces when you're browning them. If pieces touch, they steam.

- Don't overcook. A skinless, boneless breast is done if it springs back when pressed with your finger. To test other parts, pierce thickest section with a fork. Chicken is done when juices run clear. (Test on a white plate, so you can judge color.)

## Poultry Nutrition Know-How

For health-conscious and time-strapped cooks, chicken is a number-one dinner entrée. An excellent source of phosphorus and niacin and a good source of iron, zinc and riboflavin, chicken is also protein-rich. Here's a nutritional breakdown of popular poultry cuts:

*Serving size: 3-1/2 oz (100 g) cooked*

Chicken, white meat, no skin:
*173 calories, 31 g protein and 4.5 g fat*

Chicken, white meat, with skin:
*222 calories, 29 g protein and 10.9 g fat*

Chicken, dark meat, no skin:
*205 calories, 27 g protein and 9.7 g fat*

Chicken, dark meat, with skin:
*253 calories, 26 g protein and 15.8 g fat*

Wings:
*297 calories, 27 g protein and 19.8 g fat*

Ground chicken:
*227 calories, 30 g protein and 10.7 g fat*

## safety alert

**Chicken can carry harmful bacteria, so follow these guidelines:**

### Storage

- Remove store wrapping. Rinse and dry chicken. Loosely wrap in plastic or waxed paper and refrigerate for no more than three days. Or wrap in foil and freeze for up to six months.
- Refrigerate leftovers promptly. Always remove stuffing and store separately.

### Thawing

- Don't thaw frozen chicken at room temperature – bacteria will thrive.
- In refrigerator, allow four to nine hours for parts, about 16 hours for a whole bird.

- In microwave, allow three to five minutes per pound (500 grams). Cover with waxed paper and cook on defrost, rotating chicken occasionally.

### Handling

- Clean all surfaces raw chicken has touched with chlorine bleach. Give bleach one minute to work before rinsing. Use a wooden cutting board, which recent research now recommends over plastic. Clean plastic boards in the dishwasher. Do not clean a wooden board in the dishwasher. It will split.
- Wash hands after handling raw chicken.
- Wash knives used to cut raw chicken with hot soapy water before using on other foods.

index

index

index

# credits

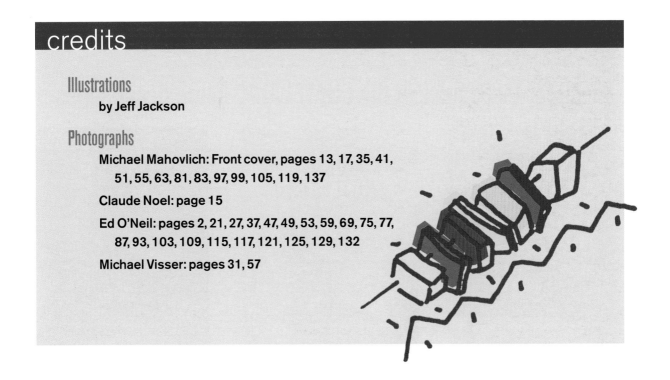

## Illustrations
**by Jeff Jackson**

## Photographs
**Michael Mahovlich: Front cover, pages 13, 17, 35, 41,
51, 55, 63, 81, 83, 97, 99, 105, 119, 137**

**Claude Noel: page 15**

**Ed O'Neil: pages 2, 21, 27, 37, 47, 49, 53, 59, 69, 75, 77,
87, 93, 103, 109, 115, 117, 121, 125, 129, 132**

**Michael Visser: pages 31, 57**

chatelaine
food express

Quickies
chicken

## For Smith Sherman Books Inc.

EDITORIAL DIRECTOR
Carol Sherman

ART DIRECTOR
Andrew Smith

SENIOR EDITOR
Bernice Eisenstein

ASSOCIATE EDITOR
Erik Tanner

PAGE LAYOUT AND COMPOSITION
Joseph Gisini, Jonathan Freeman

COLOR SEPARATIONS
T-C4 Graphics Ltd., Winnipeg

PRINTING
Kromar Printing Ltd., Winnipeg

SMITH SHERMAN BOOKS INC.
533 College Street, Suite 402,
Toronto, Canada M6G 1A8
e-mail: bloke@total.net

## For Chatelaine

FOOD EDITOR
Monda Rosenberg

TEST KITCHEN ASSISTANT
Trudy Patterson

SENIOR COPY EDITOR
Deborah Aldcorn

CHATELAINE ADVISORY BOARD
Rona Maynard, Donna Clark

DIRECTOR OF MARKETING
Mirabel Palmer-Elliot

CHATELAINE, MACLEAN HUNTER
PUBLISHING LIMITED
777 Bay Street,
Toronto, Canada M5W 1A7
e-mail: letters@chatelaine.com

# Look for these titles in the CHATELAINE home decor series

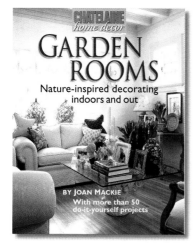

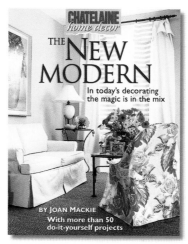

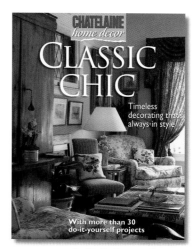

DECORATING INSPIRATION
for every room of the house,
including rooms for outdoor living
and dining, with more than
50 easy do-it-yourself projects.

SOFT MEETS SLEEK, antiques mingle
with contemporary and personal
pleasure combines with comfort
in the second book in the
CHATELAINE HOME DECOR series.

CLASSICS hold their own for
decades, even centuries, because of
their enduring beauty and timeless
charm. *Classic Chic* shows you how
to pull the look together.